LAND-USE CONTROLS
IN THE UNITED STATES

LAND-USE CONTROLS
IN THE UNITED STATES

Second Edition

JOHN DELAFONS

The M.I.T. Press
Cambridge, Massachusetts, and London, England

HD
205
1969
D4

CONTENTS

INTRODUCTION TO THE FIRST EDITION

This report was prepared during my tenure of a Harkness Fellowship of the Commonwealth Fund of New York in 1959/60. It is based on six months' work at the Joint Center for Urban Studies of M.I.T. and Harvard and at the Littauer School of Public Administration, followed by six months' travel and meetings with federal and local officials, realtors, developers, bankers, and others concerned with private development and the relationship between public and private interests in the development and redevelopment of American cities. The views expressed are my own and in no way represent those of the government department to which I belong.

This report is in six parts. Part I attempts to summarize very briefly the context in which the American system of land-use control operates: the size of the country, the pace of development, certain attitudes and preferences which influence the scope of planning, the political and economic factors which condition the methods of control, the administrative structure and the constitutional framework with which the system has to comply.

Part II describes the history of land-use controls in America. It is an interesting subject; it is also very relevant to an understanding of the system, since in the fifty years or so of its existence there has been no radical departure, nothing comparable to the fundamental reform which set the British Town and Country Planning Act of 1947 apart from planning legislation of 1909 to 1932. Nor is there any evidence that America is moving toward such a decision, despite some wishful thinking on the perimeter.

Part III outlines what seem to be the broad objectives of American planning and the motives which direct them.

Part IV describes the methods of control and gives examples of the type of standards employed. It also explains the method of administration and the appeal machinery. There is a brief account of the types of control used in urban

renewal work, where there is a contractual relationship between the public authority and the private developer. Some
examples are also given of controls employed by private
enterprise in the form of restrictive covenants and other
means of private enforcement.

Part V reviews the utility of these controls in relation to
different types of development activity and attempts to assess their effectiveness as a means of implementing a development plan. The benefits of a formalized system, subject
to judicial review, in lightening the administrative burden
and securing consistency are also considered.

Part VI draws some conclusions about the American system of land-use control and discusses certain obstacles to its
future development as an effective means of controlling the
development and redevelopment of American towns and
cities. Finally, the relevance of the American experience to
the British situation is discussed. This part of the report has
been rewritten for the purpose of American publication.

Note for British Readers

It would be sheer coincidence if governmental controls
evolved in one country could be readily adapted to the needs
of another. The American system of land-use controls, although it bears some resemblance to the type of control set
up in planning schemes under our own 1932 Act, is very
unlike our present system of control. The difference is contained in the contrast between a system of *controls* and the
simple power of *control* in section 12 of the 1947 Act. The
American system of controlling private development depends
on devising uniform standards and the avoidance of discretionary power in the hands of the planning authority.
There are historic, political, and constitutional reasons for
this. But the problem of regulating the private use of land
is not essentially different in the two democracies. What we
do in an *ad hoc* manner the Americans try to do methodi-
cally. The same type of human activity is the subject of
control, and the powers of government are not so widely
disparate. The physical conditions in a country fifty times

the size of ours obviously differ. Yet the human scale is the same—the family, the neighborhood—and in these terms the fundamental objective is the same: to ensure decent living conditions in a changing or developing community. With this much in common, the difference in methods becomes interesting and provocative.

The American system has apparently struck most English observers as antiquated, cumbersome, and ill adapted to the complexity of modern development and the demands of public policy. But it does offer an alternative to the British system, the only one which has so far been devised, and it is important to consider the utility of a more specific, and perhaps less arbitrary, system of control. The British system would be impossible without the fundamental change in property rights and the system of compensation contained in the 1947–1959 Planning Acts. Other countries may feel unwilling to make this change, or unable to meet the cost involved. The American system depends on a less radical modification of property rights (which, however, secures a considerable improvement over the laws of the jungle) and confers no claim to compensation. It is worth examining the American experience, and the current attempts to bring the system more into line with modern conditions, to see whether they offer a solution to the problem of using land to best advantage, not only in America but in other democratic countries. It would be absurd to suggest that Britain should drop her system of planning control in favor of the American model, but the comparison may throw some new light on British practices, which need to keep pace with a changing climate of opinion.

October, 1961   Middlesex, England

PREFACE TO THE SECOND EDITION

It is nearly ten years since this report on land-use controls in the United States was first written. When I was asked by the M.I.T. Press to prepare it for a second edition, I was faced with a problem: whether to attempt to bring the whole report up to date in technical terms, or whether to leave it substantially unaltered as an account of the American system of land-use controls as seen by a British observer in 1960.

Three factors led me to adopt the second alternative. First (though this did not prove so compelling a reason as it might have been) was the fact that, although I have kept in touch with American planning and planners over the years, I could not claim to have a detailed knowledge of recent technical developments in American land-use controls. Second, however, I was assured by some of my American friends that there had been no spectacular advances in those techniques since 1960, and that my account of what then appeared to be the more significant innovations remained broadly correct. It seems that developments over the past ten years have been more in the direction of wider adoption of the more modern forms of control that I had identified than toward any major change in the scope or methods of control. Third, I felt that such value as the report might have lay in its general assessments rather than in its more technical details. Its account of the historical development of American methods of land-use control—their origin and rapid growth in the 1920's and 30's, followed by a long period of stagnation and litigation, and then by a determined effort on the part of a few practicing city planners to revise and render those controls more effective—all this remained valid. The report, therefore, had a certain historical or documentary interest in itself as reflecting the state of play in American land-use controls at the end of the 1950's and the start of the 1960's, an interest which it would lose if I attempted to bring it up to date. It would also have meant attempting to do so at secondhand, rather than with that element of reportage which the original version gathered as I wrote it over the twelve months of discussion, study, and 20,000 miles travel throughout the United States in 1959/60.

But as I reread the report, ten years after it was written, I began to question how far American *attitudes* to land-use planning, as distinct from the techniques, might have changed over that decade. In 1960 there was little sign of urgent public concern with the problems of land use. Those planners who were endeavoring to alert public opinion to the dangers of unplanned and rapidly accelerating urban growth faced a largely indifferent audience. Those few planners who were convinced that, if these problems were to be dealt with at all, then the only hope was to revise, systematize, and enforce the methods of control that already existed encountered not only public indifference but also a very widespread skepticism among professional planners and academics as to the efficacy or relevance of such an approach to the problem. Transportation planning and the early bulldozer methods of urban renewal attracted far more interest than conventional land-use controls. Even those who were actively engaged in the emergent problems of urban America were more concerned—and rightly so in the wider context—with the problems of racial conflict, crime, poverty, and social deprivation rather than with the mundane, but in some ways related, questions of land-use control.

I concluded that the best course would be to leave the original report substantially unchanged and to consider, in a new chapter, how far and to what effect American attitudes to land-use planning have changed over the past decade and the extent to which these changes are reflected in the planning system. This now forms Part VII of the present edition: "Retrospect and Prospect—1969." I have also drawn attention by footnotes to some points in the original text which require modification or amplification in the light of more recent developments.

In attempting this revision without returning to the United States I have necessarily been heavily dependent on the advice of my American friends. Among these I would like to express my special thanks to Richard F. Babcock of Chicago, who is not only actively engaged in the day-to-day knockabout of zoning litigation, and one of the most entertaining writers on the subject,[1] but is also Chairman of the Advisory Committee of the American Law Institute study for a Model Land Development Code, which is engaged in a comprehensive review of the law relating to land-use controls. I discuss this review in Part VII.

Those readers who require a more detailed account of recent developments in American land-use controls may be referred to the well-organized account of the system given by Norman Williams, Jr., in *The Structure of Urban Zoning*.[2] If this book had existed when I began my study of the subject, I would have been spared a lot of arduous research. Developments in the general legislative context can be followed in the periodical legislative reviews published in the *Journal of the American Institute of Planners*.[3] The International City Managers' Association published in 1968 a new edition of their all-purpose handbook on American planning, *Principles and Practice of Urban Planning*.[4] F. Stuart Chapin produced in 1965 a new edition of his standard textbook, *Urban Land Use Planning*.[5] The political context of planning in American cities, which is critical to an understanding of how planning decisions are actually taken, is described by Alan A. Althuser in *The City Planning Process*[6] and, as part of the wider background, by Edward

1. See Richard R. Babcock, *The Zoning Game—Municipal Practices and Policies* (Madison: University of Wisconsin Press, 1966).

2. Buttenheim Publishing Corporation (New York: 1966).

3. See *Journal of The American Institute of Planners*, Vol. XXX, No. 3 (August 1964); Vol. XXXII, No. 5 (September 1966); and Vol. XXXIV, No. 5, (September 1968).

4. Edited by William I. Goodman and Eric C. Freund (Washington, D. C.: International City Managers' Association, 1968).

5. University of Illinois Press (Urbana: 1965).

6. Cornell University Press (Ithaca, N.Y.: 1965).

C. Banfield and James Q. Wilson in *City Politics*.[7] I would also recommend Christopher Tunnard's *The Modern American City*,[8] which includes a fascinating selection of readings on the subject from a wide variety of sources.

In conclusion I must emphasize that this report has a limited perspective. It is concerned primarily with land-use controls or, in the terms of my original project, the public control of private development. It does not attempt to deal in any detail with transportation planning, metropolitan planning, urban renewal, or wider aspects of urban and rural planning except insofar as they are expressed in terms of land-use control, that is, by the traditional methods of zoning and subdivision regulation. It is therefore short on the theoretical aspects of planning and on those forms of master planning or "paper planning" which are not closely related to the practical and available powers of implementation through the control of land use. I make no pretense, therefore, to appraise the real advances made in the techniques of planning—particularly notable in the application of mathematical concepts to planning problems and the development of theoretical models—or in the understanding of the social factors that contribute to the problems with which the planner attempts to deal. Those problems extend far beyond the limited range of the technical and administrative methods of control that are the subject of this report. But, and this is the theme to which I constantly recur, these methods have a contribution to make toward the solution of those problems; and there is still a danger, as there was ten years ago, that they will be neglected or dismissed as irrelevant. That is the justification for a second edition of this report.

February 1969   Hammersmith, London, England

7. Harvard University Press (Cambridge, Mass.: 1963).
8. D. Van Nostrand Company, Inc. (Princeton, N.J.: 1968).

LAND-USE CONTROLS
IN THE UNITED STATES

I CONTEXT

The Land and Its Development

Land has never been a scarce resource in America. Its great abundance has been a powerful influence on American attitudes toward the land, its development, and attempts by government to control its use. The total area of the United States (excluding Hawaii and Alaska) is 1,904 million acres. England and Wales, with a population about one quarter that of the United States, have a land area less than 2 percent of this. In an early Congressional debate on public land policies in 1796, Gallatin remarked that "If the cause of the happiness of this country was examined into, it would be found to arise as much from the great plenty of land in proportion to the inhabitants, which their citizens enjoyed, as from the wisdom of their political institutions."

The whole population of the United States could be housed within view of the Pacific Ocean. All cities and villages occupy only 10 million of the total 1,904 million acres. Of course, the fact that there are thousands of square miles of undeveloped land in, say, Arizona or Wyoming does not help the people living in metropolitan Philadelphia or New York. The population density in New Jersey and Massachusetts is greater than in most European countries. Rhode Island is almost as densely populated as the Netherlands. But the lack of any urgent concern for preserving open land as such, which has always been a dominant objective of British planning policies, is very characteristic of American attitudes. The cities of Dallas and Fort Worth are about thirty miles apart. Dallas has about 650,000 inhabitants, Fort Worth about 380,000. In the past five years the town of Arlington midway between the two has grown from 8,000 to over 40,000 and is still growing rapidly as the result of being selected by a group of New York developers for the site of Great Southwestern Industrial Estates, "the largest planned industrial development in the world." In England a similar situation would probably be met by a determined

1

attempt to keep the three communities from growing into one, and to preserve some vestige of a green belt. But there is no such concern in America. The growth of Arlington is applauded. As a Fort Worth businessman remarked to me, "Why try to stop it? In twenty minutes' drive in any direction I can be on a lake in my boat, fishing."

But the problems of land-use planning do not diminish in relation to the quantity of land. They increase in relation to the amount of development, and the pace of development in America is fantastic. The editors of *Fortune* have calculated that 3,000 acres a day are bulldozed for new development of all kinds. In England and Wales urban development takes about 30,000 acres a year. Housing production in America for the past five years has been running at the rate of about 1,300,000 units a year, of which the vast preponderance are single detached homes (and less than 2 percent are public housing). Other types of development are on a proportionate scale. In Phoenix, Arizona, from 1950–57 over 6 million square feet of shopping centers were built; 4 million square feet are under construction and 10 million are in the planning stage.

Between 1950 and 1960 the population of the United States increased by over 28 million. Bureau of Census projections for 1980 range from 230 million to 272 million, an increase over 1960 of at least 50 million and possibly nearly 100 million. At current densities the urban population of 1980 will absorb at least twice the amount of land used today. In many areas this growth can be absorbed without encroaching too noticeably on the surrounding wilderness of land. But in some regions open space has been annihilated. The Los Angeles urban area is already fifty miles wide and twenty-six miles long. By 1975 it may well have linked up the chain of settlements from Santa Barbara on the north to San Diego on the Mexican frontier, a distance equal to that from London to Manchester. Los Angeles County has grown from 3,500 persons in 1850 to over 4 million in 1950, and, incredibly, to over 6 million in 1960. Similarly, the New York conurbation is already 110 miles long, and by 1975 the east coast from Boston to Washington, a distance of over

450 miles, will probably form a single urban mass. As anyone knows who has driven route U.S. 1 between these two
cities, the effect is achieved already by the unbroken string
of roadside development. This is the "linear city" which
some see as the American norm for the future, and which
has been christened Megalopolis.

The Attitude to Growth

Despite this rampant growth, it is very rare in America to
encounter any antipathy to new development. Quite the
opposite is usually the case. We were in west Texas when
the first returns of the 1960 census were released. There was
jubilation among communities that had grown, and indigna-
tion and despondency among those that had remained static
or declined. In Sweetwater, the city council held an emer-
gency session to pass a "motion of protest" at the fact that
their population had barely shifted in the past decade.

There is general sympathy in America for the man who
builds something, and especially for the man who builds a
business. The bigger the building the more genuine the
admiration, but even the most precarious enterprise in the
most makeshift accommodation is accepted in a generous
spirit, and be the advertisements ever so blatant (they get
larger as the success of the enterprise diminishes) there is
little urge to pull them down. As Professor Brogan has observed, the average American is not the sucker who buys
wooden nutmegs but the guy who sells them.

Along with this acceptance of growth goes a thriving
speculation in land. In 1959 a book with the engaging title
*How I Turned a Thousand Dollars into a Million in Real
Estate—in My Spare Time* remained high on *The New York
Times* best seller list for thirty-eight weeks. Popular magazines advertise the attraction of investment (on hire purchase
principles) in Florida real estate—"*not* under water" runs a
reassuring phrase in the blurb. Quick fortunes are, in fact,
still made in the land market. Land in Houston that was
bought ten years ago for $400 an acre can be sold today for
$4,000 or, in some parts of the city, for $40,000. Large land-

holders are still powerful in this part of the country. One of Houston's pioneer families still owns a 60,000-acre ranch which now lies within the city limits and is being released in calculated amounts for development. Speculation in land has been a tradition in America and was in fact a major motivating force in opening the West. It was not the prerogative of the rich (none of the great American fortunes derived from real estate) but in an undeveloped country was available to all comers. This speculative bent still colors American attitudes toward the land and is a factor to be reckoned with in attempting to control its use.

Prairie Psychology

The general unconcern for the rate at which land is consumed by new development, born of the confidence that the supply is virtually unlimited, has been called the "prairie psychology." And it is not altogether fanciful to see a persistence of the log-cabin tradition in the overwhelming American preference for the detached one-story house on a large plot. The customs and attitudes of the frontier still flourish. Even thirty miles outside of Boston, small townships have all the boisterous determination to expand and the indifference to the look of things that might characterize a pioneer settlement. New businesses are welcomed, and the developer barely bothers to clear the brushwood from the site before throwing up a flimsy shelter for his trade. Within a few years it will be replaced by something more substantial, if not more permanent, or it will be pushed aside by a competitor. One of the most marked characteristics of American development is its impermanence. Even settlements which have been staging posts on major routes west for a hundred years or more show no signs of historical continuity. The gas stations, motels, and other buildings on Main Street could have been (and probably were) built within the last ten years or less. Only in towns which have outlived their original purpose—like Tombstone, Arizona, "the town too tough to die"—does the physical appearance of the frontier remain. But the attitudes of a rapidly developing community in virgin territory still prevail. Except in the old communities on the Atlantic seaboard, an aggressive individualism remains a lively reminder that people came to America as a land of opportunity. There is a real antagonism toward anyone who presumes to limit a man's right to do as he pleases with his own property. Between 1860 and 1900, 14 million immigrants entered America; between 1900 and 1940 there were 19 million. One of the fascinations of America is to see what men made of this huge country in a hundred years. The run-down, blighted neighborhoods which cover the older cities are in fact the residue of the first wave of urban settlement in the New World.

The New Mobility

The factor which has changed the whole context of development within a generation is, of course, the automobile. There are now 65 million cars on American roads. The forecast is two more cars for every three new Americans. By 1975 there will be over 100 million cars.

The result has been a revolution in the pattern of development. The location of new industry, homes, and shopping centers is no longer dependent on predictable or traditional requirements. Anything can locate anywhere, since the automobile provides the necessary link. Some new location factors are beginning to emerge, but they are not necessarily a reflection of desirable land use. The market has decided that major street intersections are the best place for shopping centers, and city planners replace the strip commercial zoning of an earlier era with an equal superfluity of commercial zones at every intersection, which from the traffic flow and safety aspects seems the worst possible location. Accessibility, which might have imposed restraint on strip development, is no longer an important factor, and nothing is more typical of the American urban scene than the marginal commercial enterprises that string out for ten or twenty miles along the approaches to major cities.

Similarly, housing need not be adjacent to shopping or

community facilities. The 1960 Parade of Homes sponsored by the Homebuilders of Houston and various utility companies and magazines (and liberally blessed by civic leaders) chose a site ten miles out of downtown Houston on a barren plain, miles from any similar development, where the only landscape feature was a flood protection ditch.

The American's idea of recreation also revolves around the car. Hunting is far more typical than hiking (despite a handful of honorable exceptions like the Appalachian Trail Club); two-thirds of all the deer taken are shot within half a mile of a main road. When the American family goes out for the day, it loads up the station wagon with fishing gear, portable barbecue, icebox, water skis, and perhaps a speed boat on a trailer, and heads at sixty miles an hour to the nearest State Park or National Forest. And these are surprisingly generous and accessible. Nearly 20 percent of California is reserved for state or national parks and forests. There are almost no neighborhood parks in which to take the dog for a walk or knock a ball about, but once in the car the most constricted urbanite is within relatively easy reach of the great outdoors.

A Barrier of Distrust

Another characteristic American attitude that exercises a fundamental influence on the methods and scope of land-use control, as on other types of governmental authority, is distrust of politicians. Americans expect corruption in government and to a remarkable degree accept it. When a recent Chicago police scandal broke (police patrol cars were being used to cart off the loot from burglarized premises), a newspaper editorial exclaimed, "There is a limit to the amount of corruption that decent citizens will tolerate." In a seminar at the Harvard Graduate School of Public Administration, the professor asserted flatly that government without corruption ("gravy") is impossible. Professor H. J. Morgenthau, writing in *The New York Times* on the payola quiz scandal, remarked that "Pecuniary corruption in the political and commercial spheres must be expected. For since the ultimate value of these fields is power, and wealth is a source of power, the possibility of pecuniary corruption is built into these spheres." Since the values conferred or denied by land-use controls are great, their administration affords exceptional opportunities for graft and by the same token exposes them to exceptionally strong pressures. The result, in America, has been a determination to eliminate the scope for discretion in land-use controls by formalizing them in a set of standard regulations and by laying down in advance the conditions under which, if at all, change may be allowed.

Free Enterprise

It is at least a basic assumption, if not entirely a fact, that the American economic system—or, as the Chambers of Commerce prefer, the American way of life—is founded on unwavering adherence to the tenets of the free market and the private enterprise system. Although the massive intervention by the federal government in, for example, agriculture or house purchase finance shows that the system is less free and less enterprising than it is usually represented, there is in fact a very strong prejudice against government control over any aspect of the economy. In matters of land planning it is generally assumed that land uses are most efficiently organized if the decisions are made by the market and the objective of control under these circumstances is simply to moderate the maladjustments of the process. The reasons why, in the face of this antipathy, land-use controls have gained the hold they have in America is discussed in Part II, and the motives and objectives of American land-use planning are further considered in Part III. It is sufficient at this stage to note the dominance of this economic credo, and to observe that one important result is that American planners are much more diffident about interfering with the process of private development and the choices made by the market mechanism than British planners have been.

Agriculture

No one in America feels any great concern for protecting agricultural land from urban development. The government's problem has been to hold down farm production. For twenty-five years farmers have been subject to restrictions on acreage but have been protected by a massive price support system which is currently costing the government $9 billion. The alternative policy now favored is to extend greatly the land retirement program which dates back to 1933. Under this system the government "rents" land from farmers for five- to ten-year periods and places it in a conservation reserve or "soil bank." From 1956–59, some 22,-500,000 acres were removed from production by this method. The aim is to adjust supply more nearly to demand, and remove the need for government storage, quotas, or price support except when sudden collapse threatens. Agricultural economists stress that to be really effective the soil bank must attract highly productive farms and not merely the marginal or inefficient ones.

If the farmer can sell his land to a builder, that is so many acres less to burden the soil bank. In the New England region, despite the vast amount of development in the past ten years, the amount of unused land has actually increased. The farmer finds it more profitable to sell out to speculators and retire to Florida or move west to the farm belt; the land remains idle until suburbanization catches up with it.

In a few areas, where specialist crops are grown and the productive value of land is very high, there have been attempts to protect it by adapting urban land-use controls to the needs of the agricultural community; these are described in Part IV.

Local Government

Planning and land-use control are carried out by municipalities, incorporated units of local government. There were 3,164 municipalities in the United States in 1952. Other powers of local government are divided among the municipalities and a bewildering array of unincorporated units, school districts, and special districts—ad hoc authorities, usually serving one purpose (fire protection, drainage, soil conservation, etc.).

None of the 168 standard metropolitan areas is governed by a single, all-purpose authority. In 1900 there were 1,521 cities in these areas; by 1950, 1,354 new cities had been created, and half of these were in only sixteen areas. The five largest metropolitan areas include 748 municipalities. The total number of local government units in these five areas is even more bewildering:

New York	1,071
Chicago	960
Philadelphia	702
Pittsburgh	616
St. Louis	420

The next six areas in size have around 300 authorities apiece.

There are no effective planning authorities covering more than one local government unit; each municipality is its own planning agency, and the power of land-use control is one activity which is never relinquished to another authority. Inevitably it is made to serve essentially local interests, and, by very general admission, private interests are more likely to be observed than any conscious public objective. The reasons for this and the relationship between public and private interests (which are not necessarily contradictory) are considered in Part III.

Outside the incorporated areas, the counties may exercise similar planning powers to those of the cities. This is a comparatively recent development; ten years ago only a handful of states granted zoning and subdivision control powers to the counties; now all states but one have granted powers to at least some of their counties. This is important since, despite the flood of incorporations, the population of unincorporated parts of the standard metropolitan areas has increased much more rapidly than that of incorporated areas. A few of the more urban counties have developed the controls available to the cities, and in a very few cases joint city-county regulations have been adopted. But the county planning function does not survive incorporation, and all powers of land-use control pass to the municipality whether its population is 50,000 or 500.

Whatever the effect of this multiplicity of units on the efficiency and economy of local government and its services (many cities contract with the county for all their services, simply retaining for themselves the right to say yes or no —particularly in matters of land-use), the effect is to render impossible any consistent or widely based planning policies for the metropolitan area.

There are a handful of "Regional Planning Authorities" of an advisory character set up on an ad hoc basis by state legislatures, but none have any powers of control and their influence seems to be minimal. In the 1930's an attempt was made to build up state planning agencies but they disintegrated in nearly every state during the war years. More recently they have been revived as part of the federal government's policy for administering its grants in aid for planning by smaller communities, but they exert little authority and only one or two engage in state-wide planning studies.[1]

Finally, the role of the federal government in land-use planning is at the present time insignificant and intentionally so. During the New Deal the National Resources Planning Board carried out a major program of research which demonstrated the inadequacy of traditional land-use controls and the need for plans and policies to guide the use of available controls. But the antagonism to any suggestion of federal dominance in what is regarded as essentially a local concern has defeated more recent legislative attempts to establish a "Department of Urbiculture" that would give Cabinet status to urban affairs.[2] Even where the federal

1. There has since been a revival of interest in the state governments as planning agencies, and the Department of Housing and Urban Development is encouraging the formation of metropolitan planning agencies. See Part VII.

2. The Department of Housing and Urban Development, with Cabinet status, became the eleventh executive department of the United States Government on 9th September 1965. See Part VII.

government under its "701 program" contributes half the cost of preparing master plans for smaller communities (under 25,000 population) administration of the program is left to the state planning agencies and no requirements are laid down even for the contents or character of such a plan. Similarly, federal officials emphasize that the urban renewal program (in which the federal government pays two-thirds of the net cost of the project) is a "local program locally administered." In fact the federal agency plays an important part in the program, but it is true that the important decisions are left to the local authority, and the initiative rests entirely with them. The Housing and Home Finance Agency exercises far more influence over the institutions of private enterprise (the mortgage market and the homebuilding industry) than it does over local governments.

Organization for Planning

Although every municipality has the power to control land use and private development, the decision may be to do without it. There is no obligation to exercise control (unless the city wants to participate in the federal urban renewal program) and although most communities of any size have adopted a rudimentary zoning ordinance, the chances are that it will be thirty years or more out of date and be readily amended to admit any new tax-producing development. But even the rudiments are by no means universal. Of the 1,378 cities of over 10,000 population listed in the *Municipal Year Book,* only 791 had comprehensive zoning ordinances in 1953. Subdivision control, which is regarded by many planning officials as a more effective control was used in only 509 of those cities. The total may well have increased since that date, but there are certainly many communities which get along without any public control over private land use.

The planning agency within the city government has traditionally been a city planning commission appointed by the mayor from among leading citizens, not themselves members of the council. The commission has usually been vested

with power to advise in the planning and programming of
public improvements, and responsibility for administering
the subdivision regulations which usually allow little scope
for discretion. The commission has generally also been
charged with preparing a "Master plan," which is not so
much a plan for land use as a broad picture of how the city
might improve itself by a program of public works. The
city council often reserves to itself the most influential function—that of approving changes in the zoning map, on
which the planning commission might or might not be in-
vited to comment. The planning commission has generally
been expected and disposed to remain "above politics."
Consequently it has never exerted much influence in city
government or in major development decisions. More recently planning has begun to assume an important place in
city management partly because of the need to control both
public and private development, partly because it can serve
a useful coordinating function, and partly because politicians saw in it a source of good publicity which they were
reluctant to leave to the ineffective planning commission.
It is very clear that many city planning departments, particularly those with a lavish budget and the glossiest publications, serve primarily as a public relations service for the
city government—or, in the parlance, "front men for the
mayor." Planning staffs are absorbed into the managerial
hierarchy and the planning commission usually survives in
an even more exiguous position than before. Its survival,
even in this attenuated form, only serves to obscure the
proper role of planning as an executive arm of government,
and to blur the relationship between the planning function
and political responsibility.

Finally, land-use control, like every other activity of government in America, has to stand the test of the Constitution as interpreted by the courts. Whereas in Britain land-
use planning remains entirely within the control of the
executive and legislature, in America the courts, not a
Minister, are the final arbiters in disputed decisions. The
courts will not substitute their judgment for that of the
locally appointed body, provided that it has not acted un-

reasonably or gone beyond its acknowledged authority. But the American attorney is a resourceful character and the amount of litigation on planning decisions is formidable. Any student of the American system of land-use control can soon find himself sunk in a deluge of ingenious law journal articles from which there is no recovery.

The Outer Limits of Control

A crucial difference between the American and British systems of land-use controls is that in America no compensation is payable to owners whose property loses value as the result of a planning decision.

In very brief outline, the British system confers compensation only where the land affected by the planning decision had development value before the present system of control was introduced.[3] If the land has acquired development value since then, no compensation is payable except where the decision cancels "existing use" rights. If, however, the land has become "incapable of reasonably beneficial use" as a result of a planning decision, then the owner can require the local authority to purchase the land. The compensation position in Britain and America is now somewhat similar, i.e. in general, no compensation for planning decisions. But whereas in Britain the introduction of the control system was accompanied by massive compensation (a fund of £300 million was established for the purpose), in America the system has never been accompanied by any provision for compensation. It is essential to understand the reasons for this, since the lack of power to pay compensation, and the absence of any "once and for all" settlement on the

3. The system introduced in Britain in 1947 also provided that persons wishing to carry out development should purchase the development value of the land from the state by paying a "development charge." This attempt to recoup betterment to offset the cost of compensation was abandoned in 1952, but a similar charge was introduced by the Land Commission Act 1967. The position now is that the developer generally has to pay a betterment levy if he obtains planning permission to develop his land but he gets no compensation if he is refused permission (except in the cases already referred to).

lines of the British system, obviously curtails the scope of land-use control in America.

The originators of the zoning system in America had to decide on which of two quite distinct governmental powers these new controls should be based: eminent domain or the police power. If property rights were condemned under the power of eminent domain (compulsory acquisition), then compensation would have to be paid. If on the other hand these controls could be brought under the police power (the general residual power of government to pass laws in the interests of the general public health, safety, and welfare), then no compensation would be payable and the controls would be analogous to fire or structural regulations. Casting its shadow over this problem, and causing the lawyers involved in this long debate to move with extreme caution, has been the Fifth Amendment: "No person . . . shall be deprived of life, liberty, or property, without due process of law; nor shall private property be taken for public use without just compensation."

This was the key problem facing the Commission on the Height of Buildings which was set up in 1913 to advise the city of New York on the means of controlling private development. The commission's report is a basic document in the history of American planning. The choice facing the Commission was an extremely difficult one, but they had no doubt about the answer. In practical terms proceeding by the slow and cumbrous method of eminent domain was impossible, and though the limits of the police power in this field were almost uncharted, it was the only hope of securing simple and uniformly effective control. The Commission concluded:

It is theoretically conceivable that a general plan of building restriction and regulation might be entered upon by resort to the power of eminent domain, but, practically, such a resolution is out of the question. The expense and burden of condemnation proceedings and litigation in multitudinous cases would create a tax burden that would increase rather than compensate for the injury to property interests. Moreover, the kinds of regulation under consideration are not such as to justify individual compensation. While they restrict individual liberty to a certain extent, they do it in such a way as to conserve individual and public interests and rights. They subject the use of urban land to such restrictions as are appropriate and reasonable in the nature and history of this class of property.

This decision determined the direction and limits of planning controls in America. The controls had to be such as would not justify compensation to individual owners, and they must bear a clearly demonstrable relation to the public health, safety, or welfare. There was no knowing how the courts might interpret this relation, but it was clear that the controls could not extend very far beyond the basic objectives of separating out grossly incompatible uses and establishing minimum standards of development.

II HISTORY

The Right to Develop

The land policies of the British government contributed
their share to the causes of the American Revolution. In
1763 King George attempted to arrest the advance westward across the Alleghenies by forbidding settlements beyond the sources of the rivers flowing into the Atlantic. The
vast land grants to aristocratic absentee landlords and the
attempt to establish a feudal manorial system in the colonies
sowed the seeds of revolt. During and after the War of
Independence the great estates granted by the Crown were
taken over by the states and redistributed mostly in small
holdings. The Fairfax estate of six million acres in Virginia
and Lord Granville's holdings covering a third of North
Carolina were dismembered. Following the political revolution the last vestiges of antique property laws were dis-
carded. Primogeniture, which was not finally ended in Britain until 1925, was abolished in every state in the Union by
1800. Leasehold estates were almost unknown. Even the
great plantations of the South were run by their proprietors
rather than by a subordinate tenantry. Freehold land ownership became the accepted right of the citizen.

This dominance of the private landowner, however, was
not automatic. Nearly all the land in the United States was
at some stage publicly owned, much of it by the federal
government. Following confiscation of the Crown lands, the
thirteen states in the years 1780–90 ceded a large proportion of their western territory to the federal government. In
the following half century vast new lands were added by
purchase or treaty. The Louisiana Purchase alone added
over 500 million acres in 1803.

These lands were initially the property of the people of
the United States. This was the "public domain" which at its
largest, excluding Alaska, covered about 1,425 million acres
—nearly three-quarters of the whole country. From the
early days of independence through the first half of the

16

nineteenth century, debate raged over the proper management of these public lands. On one side John Quincy Adams and others struggled to secure compact settlement of the land and to make it a source of public benefit as well as private profit. On the other side, Jefferson, Benton, and Andrew Jackson urged the policy of rapid and extensive settlement, to build a nation of individual freeholders. Despite the doubts expressed about the wisdom of unrestricted exploitation and unlimited dispersion, as opposed to progressive settlement, the public demand for free access to the land was overwhelming. John Quincy Adams was obliged to confess, "My own system of administration, which was to make the national domain the inexhaustible fund for progressive improvement, has failed."

Government regarded land as the most readily available source of revenue and made it available to all who were hardy enough to take it. Apart from establishing a simple and reliable system of land registration and transfer and the rectilinear system of surveying introduced in 1785 (which left its characteristic checkerboard pattern over all the settlements of the West), the government exercised little or no control over development of the land. Gradually even the price on land was removed. The Homestead Act of 1862 granted plots of 160 acres to any settler who would build a house, live on the land, and farm part of it for five years. Over 1,400,000 homesteads were established on more than 247 million acres of the public domain. The Oklahoma Territory was opened for settlement on April 22, 1889, with an Army cavalryman's gunshot—the signal for several thousand land-hungry pioneers who had gathered on the border to stampede into the new country. By nightfall every inch of the two million acres had been staked for claim, or so the story goes.

The possibility of orderly development was not entirely ignored at the local level. The act of founding a new settlement in the wilderness emphasized both the dependence of the individual upon the success of the town as a whole and the importance of planning for the expected growth and future of the community. In the eighteenth and early nineteenth centuries several towns were founded with the intention of planned development—Savannah, Georgia; Manchester, New Hampshire; Paterson, New Jersey; Reading, Pennsylvania; Buffalo, New York; Madison, Wisconsin; Detroit, Michigan; Annapolis, Maryland; Williamsburg, Virginia, and, of course, Washington, D. C. But in nearly every case the plan was either not carried beyond the initial stages or was swamped by later development. American land-use controls cannot be traced to an ideological preference for the planned community. There is nothing utopian about those controls, and their origin is to be found not in a theory of town planning but in the common law of nuisance and in the public statutes regulating noxious industries.

The Right to Protect and Control

The right to own and develop land free from government interference became a key dogma in the American economic credo. "We hold these truths to be self-evident, that all men are created equal, that they are endowed by their Creator with certain inalienable Rights, that among these are Life, Liberty and the pursuit of Happiness," affirmed the Declaration of Independence in 1776, to which the state of Massachusetts added in 1780 words which were subsequently written into many state constitutions: "the right of . . . acquiring, possessing and protecting property."

With this devotion to the rights of property among a nation of individual freeholders, coupled with an unwavering adherence to the tenets of the free market and private enterprise, one would expect to find in America a formidable antipathy to any government control over private development. But government has exercised continuous and often elaborate control over many facets of private enterprise and private development since colonial days. The Council of the Dutch Colony laid down in 1625 the type and location of houses that might be built in New Amsterdam, nearly 300 years before New York adopted what is now regarded as the first comprehensive zoning ordinance. The town of Cambridge soon after its founding in the Massachusetts Bay Colony required that "Houses shall range even and stand just six feet in their own ground from the street."

Americans have interpreted the right of "protection" of property to mean protection not only (or even primarily) from impingement by government but also from impingement by competing private interests. For example, the interest conserved may be that of private property owners against both speculative developers and unwanted newcomers, or it may be the dominance of a private developer over less influential private interests. The precedents and development of American land-use controls illustrate these tendencies.

It is a very significant fact that the American system of regulating private development—"zoning"—is a legàcy of the 1920's, the heyday of free enterprise. In 1919 only twenty cities had adopted a zoning ordinance; by 1929 the total was 973. The system and its potentialities can be understood only by going back to its origins in the age of Coolidge, and by discovering the motives for establishing the system and what its originators hoped to achieve.

The Progress of Zoning

The earliest examples of zoning are those introduced in California toward the end of the nineteenth century as a means of discriminating against Chinese immigrants. After several attempts at statutory discrimination had been held to be unconstitutional, San Francisco seized upon the fact that the Chinese laundries, many of which were flourishing social centers, were a clear fire risk and public nuisance. In 1885 the city banned public laundries from most areas, thereby putting nearly three hundred Chinese laundries out of business. The city's right to impose such restrictions was upheld by the California courts in 1886 in the cases of Yick Wo and Hang Kie. Typical of these early zoning laws is the ordinance adopted by the city of Modesto in 1885:

It shall be unlawful for any person to establish, maintain, or carry on the business of a public laundry or wash house where articles are washed and cleansed for hire, within the city of Modesto, except that part of the city which lies west of the railroad track and south of G street.

The "wrong side of the tracks" was thus given statutory definition in the earliest land-use controls.

After the success with laundries, San Francisco restricted dance halls, livery stables, slaughterhouses, saloons, pool halls, and other potential nuisances. A few years later Los Angeles established the districting device on a comprehensive basis. In a series of ordinances from 1909–1915 the city was divided into twenty-seven districts in which all kinds of industry were permitted, about a hundred "residence exception" districts in which all but heavy and noxious industries were allowed, and a single large zone restricted to residential use. The principle of controlling land use by districts was found to be a convenient way of protecting residential districts without the troublesome and expensive litigation required to obtain injunctive relief against nuisances.

Meanwhile a similar device had been developed on the east coast for regulating the height and bulk of buildings. In 1885 the state of New York limited the height of tenements to one and a half times the street width. In 1889 Congress restricted the height of buildings in parts of Washington. In 1898 Massachusetts restricted buildings around Copley Square in Boston to a height of 90 feet and, which was unusual, provided for compensation to affected owners. By 1913 twenty-two cities had height control, but only Milwaukee, Boston, Washington, and Indianapolis combined their control with some form of districting. In all cities except Washington the limit was at least 125 feet, and in Milwaukee it was 225 feet.

In 1913 the city of New York, following a grant of power from the state, began to develop the first comprehensive zoning ordinance. This is the major landmark in the evolution of land-use controls in America. The best legal minds in the field worked on the ordinance, and it naturally served as a model for the great spate of ordinances which were produced in the next decade. The origins and character of New York's pioneer work is worth looking at in some detail. The decisions and choices made by New York in 1913–16 proved definitive. Except in a few leading cities that have substantially revised their zoning ordinances in recent years, this early model continues to be followed. The current question in America is, how far can the system to which the country was committed in 1916–1929 be adapted to meet the planning problems and policies of the next decade?

The arrival of the skyscraper forced New York to take the lead in instigating land-use controls. By 1913 there were over fifty buildings in Manhattan of more than twenty stories and nine above thirty stories. The highest was fifty-five stories. The concentration of tall buildings downtown, shutting off light and air from many older properties, caused growing concern and resentment. For example, the Equitable Building at 120 Broadway, which covered a solid city block to the height of thirty-eight stories, cast its shadow over seven acres of adjacent property. Something had to be done if property values in New York were not to be concentrated in a bunch of skyscraper office buildings below which all was darkness. A group of property owners, the Fifth Avenue Association, took the initiative in 1911. The members were concerned not only by the loss of light and air, but also by the low-paid workers who poured out of the skyscrapers onto lower Fifth Avenue at the end of the workday, ruining what was once a fashionable shopping district. They feared that these conditions would spread up the famous Avenue. Pressure from these property owners led to establishment of the Advisory Commission on the Height of Buildings in 1913. The chairman was Edward M. Bassett, one of the lawyers who acted as midwives to the birth of zoning in America. Within a year the commission produced its report, which is a basic document in the history of American land-use control.

The commission found "conclusive evidence of the need of greater public control over building development." It said that "the present almost unrestricted power to build to any height, over any proportion of the lot, for any desired use and in any part of the city, has resulted in injury to real estate and business interests, and to the health, safety and general welfare of the city."

The restrictions recommended by the commission were briefly:

1. No building should be higher than twice the width of the street, but no limit was to be less than 100 feet nor more than 300 feet.
2. Above the maximum height, building might continue with one foot setback for each 4 feet of increase in height.
3. Above the first story 10 percent of interior lot should be left vacant.
4. Side and back courts should be a depth equal to 1¼ times the number of stories above the first (e.g. a 21-story building would require courts 25 feet deep). The minimum depth was six feet.
5. A tower should be allowed to any height, covering not more than 25 percent of the lot area and set back 20 feet from lot and street lines.

The commission recognized that its proposals were "so liberal as to be practically no force in controlling actual building development except in very limited areas throughout the city." It therefore recommended that further study be made of the possibility of dividing the city into districts, with regulations to meet the needs of each type of district and to control the location of each type of use.

A second commission was formed on Building Districts and Restrictions, again with Bassett as chairman. This commission took two years to report, and viewed more liberally the case for controlling private development. In a preliminary report of March 1916, the commission declared that

New York city has certainly reached a point beyond which continued unplanned growth cannot take place without inviting social and economic disaster. It is too big a city, the social and economic interests involved are too great to permit the continuance of the laissez faire methods of earlier days. There is too much at stake to permit a habit of thought as to private property rights to stand in the way of a plan that is essential to the health, order and welfare of the entire city and to the conservation of property values.

This willingness to modify private property rights in the name of defending property values is characteristic of the early protagonists of zoning. In fact the conservation of property values or, as the commission's earlier report put it, "the character of the district," was the bedrock of zoning arguments.

The commission recommended three types of zoning district: residential, business, and unrestricted. Separate height and bulk districts were also recommended with more detailed restrictions. The city quickly adopted the commission's scheme. This ordinance of 1916 remained in force until 1961. It was amended more than 2,000 times.

This first comprehensive zoning ordinance was crude, lax, too much concerned with conserving existing values, and too little concerned with guiding future growth and development. It made excessive provision for business use, zoning the frontage of every major street for business except in the extreme outlying areas, where only alternate streets were so designated. The height limit was nowhere less than the street width, which meant that even in suburban Brooklyn residential buildings could go up to eight or nine stories, or higher with a setback. Perhaps the most serious defect was the failure to match the exclusion of industry from residential areas with exclusion of residences from business or industrial areas. The one substantial advantage of the zoning system—preventing confused and incompatible development—was thus severely compromised.

The authors of the ordinance were handicapped by uncertainty over what the courts would approve. The constitutionality of zoning restrictions on private property had not then been tested in the New York courts, and a case did not reach the Supreme Court of the United States until 1926. If the commissioners had been bolder, they might have alarmed property owners and jeopardized their chance of success. The Commission remarked in its 1916 report, "In city building, as in most things, even a poor plan is better than no plan at all."

The "City Beautiful" crusade which was sparked off by the Chicago Exhibition of 1892 had certain affinities with the more prosaic zoning movement. A desire for orderliness and eradication of the appalling muddle which characterized American cities was common to both. Roughly speaking, the pioneers in American town planning comprised the architects on one side obsessed with a Beaux-Arts ideal of civic beauty, and the lawyers on the other working with almost equal obsession on the task of formulating a practical system of land-use control and a legal theory to sustain it. The lawyers had more success than the architects, and their work has been called "a major achievement of the American bar." But the lack of any substantial relationship between the legal machinery and a clear concept of city planning is the firmest impression left by the origin and later course of land-use control in America. The problem of guiding zoning through its ordeals in the courts was the main preoccupation at first. All the great luminaries of the early days of zoning were lawyers: Edward Bassett, Alfred Bettman, James Metzenbaum, F. B. Williams. Given the nature of American institutions and attitudes, it may have been inevitable that lawyers rather than architects or professional planners should have been the successful pioneers of land-use controls. They thought in terms of modifying traditional legal concepts of property rather than in terms of planning problems and objectives. Similarly, it was as a means of strengthening the institution of private property in the face of rapid and unsettling changes in the urban scene that zoning won such remarkable acceptance in American communities.

The census of 1920 revealed that for the first time in American history more people lived in urban than in rural areas. During the next decade zoning became a familiar and permanent part of the American scene. Table I shows the rate of progress:

Table I Zoning Ordinances Adopted by American Cities. 1915–1937

Year	Cumulative Total	Annual Total
1915	5	1
1916	8	3
1917	12	4
1918	13	1
1919	20	7
1920	35	15
1921	78	43
1922	184	106
1923	292	108
1924	368	76
1925	484	116
1926	591	107
1927	706	115
1928	833	127
1929	973	140
1930	1100	127
1931	1195	95
1932	1236	41
. . .	. . .	
1937	1322	
. . .	. . .	
(1959: 875 cities over 10,000 population)		

In 1921 Secretary of Commerce Herbert Hoover set up an Advisory Committee on Zoning that issued a Standard State Zoning Enabling Act. This act was widely adopted. The first printed edition in 1924 sold 50,000 copies. In a preface to this document, the future President wrote, "The discovery that it is practical by city zoning to carry out reasonable neighborly agreements as to the use of land has made an almost instant appeal to the American people."

The constitutionality of the system, however, had still to meet the test of the United States Supreme Court. In 1908 the Court had observed that "Our social system rests largely upon the sanctity of private property." In a period when the Court was rejecting attempts to regulate the wages of women in industry as an invasion of personal liberty, it seemed uncertain whether zoning would survive scrutiny.

That a department of the federal government had issued a standard enabling act composed by the best legal draftsmen available and adopted by more than twenty state legislatures, endowed it with no finality. The test came in 1926. At that time zoning ordinances had been upheld by the highest courts of eleven states. Adverse decisions had been rendered in Mississippi, New Jersey, Maryland, and Georgia.

The case that reached the Supreme Court was *Village of Euclid v. Ambler Realty Co.* A severer test for zoning could hardly have been devised. The merits of the case were certainly dubious, and the damage to private property values was impressive. The area in question was sixty-eight acres. About half the land was zoned for industrial use and the other half residential, with a narrow "buffer zone" between the two for apartment houses, etc. The owners wanted the whole area zoned for industry. It was agreed that the value of the land for industrial use was $10,000 an acre against only $2,500 an acre for residential use. After the first argument the court was apparently disposed to find that zoning was an unconstitutional invasion of property rights. But at a rehearing, Alfred Bettman brilliantly argued the case for zoning. Conscious of the Court's conservatism, he argued that "zoning represents no radically new type of property regulation, but merely a new application of sanctioned traditional methods for sanctioned traditional purposes." But he did not overstress the analogy with nuisance law; instead he emphasized that the aim of zoning was to secure "general orderliness" in cities and to afford "environmental protection." However, Mr. Justice Sutherland, in delivering the opinion of the Court, relied heavily on the nuisance analogy, coining the classic phrase, "A nuisance may be merely the right thing in the wrong place,—like a pig in the parlor instead of the barnyard." He concluded:

If these reasons, thus summarized, do not demonstrate the wisdom or sound policy of those restrictions which we have indicated as pertinent to the inquiry, at least, the reasons are sufficiently cogent to preclude us from saying, as it must be said before the ordinance can be declared unconstitutional, that such provisions are clearly arbitrary and unreasonable, having no substantial relation to the public health, safety, morals or general welfare.

The constitutionality of zoning was thus firmly established and, apart from the Nectow case in 1928 (when the Court without invalidating the ordinance refused to support the zoning of a particular lot), the Supreme Court has never had occasion to reexamine its views on zoning. The Court has consistently refused to pass judgment on zoning cases and has simply denied petitions for certiorari or dismissed the appeal without elaborating its reasons. This has not meant that zoning has had an easy passage in the state courts. Judges have not hesitated to find particular applications of zoning unreasonable and invalid uses of the police power, while accepting the Supreme Court's ruling that the device itself is constitutional. Generally speaking, the courts have continued to find comfort in the analogies with nuisance law on which Justice Sutherland relied, and in the belief that zoning preserves property values.

Subdivision Control

Zoning, on account of certain legal inhibitions and the terms on which it won acceptance, has seldom (if ever) been used effectively to guide the pace and location of new development. A potentially more effective tool for this purpose is subdivision control—the regulations which specify the conditions for dividing undeveloped land into lots and offering it for sale. The basis for subdivision control is land registration, a privilege that the government has power to grant or withhold on its own terms. The land recording system set up after the Revolution dealt only with the mechanical and legal details of the registry of deeds and survey methods. Gradually regulation of street widths and other details of layout was introduced. The earliest example was in 1882, when the village of Oak Park, Illinois, required plats to be filed in advance of sale and to conform to certain standards of layout. But subdivision controls were not thought of as a means of limiting the amount of development until the vast land speculations of the 1920's showed the folly and ruinous expense to local governments of unrestricted subdivision. In this decade, when zoning controls were being adopted, practically no control was exercised over the amount of land seized for development. In Florida enough land was subdivided to house the population of the entire United States. In northern Westchester County in New York State and along the New Jersey coast, thousands of twenty-foot lots were distributed by newspapers as free gifts to new subscribers. The result was that vast quantities of land on the outskirts of every large town and city were roughly hewn up for development with jerry-built homes and without proper roads, water, schools, and other city services.

The wastage of land was appalling. In 1929 of 375,000 registered lots in Cleveland, 175,000 were vacant. In 1934 there was said to be enough vacant platted land in the country to house 18 million people. A slump in the building industry put an end to this frantic process, and a long period followed during which the effects of the "orphaned subdivision" and the cost to the community of random, uncontrolled development could be studied at leisure. When the next suburban building boom began after the second World War, communities were prepared to use subdivision regulations to exert at least a modicum of control. In some communities such controls were used, along with zoning, to make it very difficult for profitable development to take place. Generally speaking, subdivision controls have had an easier passage in the courts than zoning, and the possibility of their use as a more positive restraint on new development is being actively canvassed.

The Use and Abuse of the System

The main reason for the popularity of zoning was that it maintained the character of the best residential districts, or, in the case of smaller towns and villages, of the whole community, by severely restricting the scope for new development or changes in the intensity and type of use of existing property. The object of zoning was often said to be ensuring the "stability" of neighborhoods or small communities. The close link between the early California ordinances and racial segregation has already been described. Open attempts to use zoning for this purpose were struck down by the United States Supreme Court in 1917 when it condemned an ordinance excluding Negroes from certain districts in Louisville, Kentucky. But more or less obvious "segregation ordinances" came before the courts as late as 1949. Even if these flagrant breaches of the Fourteenth Amendment proved abortive, it is true that zoning permits a degree of social and economic segregation impossible to achieve by any other method. It can also afford protection to the small community that wants to guard against unlimited growth of any kind. Ordinances which surround the existing settlement in small towns with zones restricted to a minimum lot size of two, three, or even five acres are common. The remarkable popularity of zoning with small communities is shown by the statistics: of the 1,236 ordinances in force in 1932, 563 were for towns of 1,000 to 10,000 inhabitants, and ninety-three were for villages of less than 1,000.

At the other extreme, many zoning ordinances adopted by the larger cities in the 1920's reflected the exuberant confidence of that decade in future growth and business prosperity. These ordinances were predicated on maximum development, and many property owners and real estate promoters insisted on allocation of their land for commercial and industrial uses in the confident belief that this would automatically enhance its value. They were abetted by an influential group of professional planners who argued that zoning must reflect whatever use the land seemed best adapted for, and that if scattered commercial development existed it must be assumed that all land in the vicinity was equally well adapted for such development. The result was vast overzoning. The Boston zoning ordinance adopted in 1924 allotted 25 percent of the city for industry although only 2½ percent was at that time in industrial use. Information collected by the National Resources Committee in its 1939 report on *Urban Planning and Land Policies* contrasted

the areas zoned for various uses in major American cities
with the land actually in use for those purposes. The commercial zones were up to five times, and the residential allocation up to thirty times, the area then in use for those
purposes. Conversely, in St. Louis one-third of the land in
residential use was rezoned for commercial or industrial use.
The Committee also recorded the results of a survey made
by *The American City* in 1936 which showed that in several
cities the zoning regulations allowed a developer to erect
on a one-acre site a building of over 4,000,000 cubic feet; in
Nashville, Tennessee, the maximum was 6,500,999 cubic
feet. A building of this density has never been built. The
same survey showed that cities that specified the maximum
number of families per acre in residential districts allowed
69 to 216 *families* per acre.

By 1931 a good deal of disenchantment with the whole
zoning system was setting in among the original supporters
of zoning. This has persisted, at least in academic circles, to
the present time. Reviewing the craze for zoning in a special
issue of *The Annals of the American Academy of Political
and Social Science* in 1931, Gordon Whitnall gloomily concluded that "All of the painstaking care that typified the
early stages of the subject seems now to have established a
foundation of ignorant confidence in the extent of permissible regulation that bids fair to undo all of the careful
preparation that was made."

As early as 1924 Clarence Stein, one of the few outstanding planners America has produced and the creator with
Henry Wright of Radburn and the Greenbelt towns, came
out with as vigorous and perceptive a criticism of the zoning
system as has ever been made. Speaking at the American
Institute of Architects' annual convention, he commented
that the initial justification for zoning was to avoid the
blighting of residential areas by industrial and business use,
but that in practice:

zoning immediately passed beyond the matter of conserving that
which would accrue to the advantage of the common welfare

and proceeded to utilize the principle and the power to conserve, stabilize and enhance property values . . .

If we turn back to the original concept it is clear that zoning as it is now carried on can hardly be justified on the ground that, by and large, it serves the interest of the common welfare. It may be that the segregation of economic classes is quite the reverse.

On the other hand, from the standpoint of the architect, zoning has imposed innumerable restrictions, many of them futile and unimportant, which tend to increase the complexity of his task in planning for the use of property, often preventing the introduction of desirable innovations suggested by intelligent appreciation of his problem.

In sum, the only rational end for which zoning can exist, namely, to promote better communities for living and working and bringing up children, is actually often hindered by the present applications of zoning.

The misapplication of zoning controls, their use to serve private interests, restrictions so ample as not to be restrictions at all, or restrictions so harsh as to exclude or segregate unwanted newcomers or minorities—all these need not invalidate the principles of zoning and other land-use controls. But knowledge of their misuse has brought them into disrepute among many persons concerned with urban problems and land-use planning. Their utility as a means of implementing more positive planning policies is considered later in Part V. The important point is that their usefulness is conditioned, in America at least, by the use which has been made of them in the past, by the interests that won acceptance of them in communities large and small, and by the intimate relationship that has developed between these controls and private property rights—so that many property owners have come to feel a vested interest in what was originally seen as an unprecedented invasion of those ancient rights.

III OBJECTIVES

The Functions of Control

The demands made on the American system of land-use control, and the results expected of it, are far less than those which the British system was designed to serve. In the absence of any national policies for urban land use, and in view of a quite different governmental concern in matters of agricultural land use, there is no attempt to regulate on a national scale the distribution of industry, population, or employment, to keep agricultural land in production or to preserve open country. Nor is there generally any desire to exert stringent control over the way things look.

The primary purpose of American land-use controls, under the police power, has been to promote (in the words of the traditional formula) the "health, safety, morals, and general welfare" of the community. They have been aimed at preventing the worst effects of uncontrolled urban and industrial development by establishing certain standards of compatibility, density, light, air, and space. They were in the tradition of health and safety codes, and many of the controls could equally well have found a place there. The big difference was that these new controls set up different standards for different neighborhoods, instead of minimum standards for the whole city. This was what some of the early and soundest critics of zoning found most difficult to swallow. How could one justify, as an objective of official regulations, higher standards of light and air in some parts of the city than in others? These criticisms were brushed aside, but it has always been one of the basic weaknesses of zoning controls that they purported to be based on health and safety considerations when in fact they were aimed at preserving and fostering a wide range of living conditions.

Apart from these regulatory objectives, zoning has also been aimed explicitly at protecting and promoting the value of private property. The general attitude of local legislators

32

̇ a enacting zoning ordinances, and of the courts in uphold-
ing them, was bluntly stated by the New Jersey Superior
Court in *Borough of Cresskill v. Borough of Dumont* in
1953:

Zoning ordinances can only prohibit a use which would be harmful to other property. And, in order to be valid, zoning restrictions and limitations must have a tendency to promote the general welfare by prohibiting in particular areas, uses which would
be detrimental to the full enjoyment of the established use for
the property in that area. *The real object, however, of promoting
the general welfare by zoning ordinances is to protect the private
use and enjoyment of property and to promote the welfare of the
individual property owner. In other words, promoting the general welfare is a means of protecting private property.*

American land-use controls, in effect, were designed to
promote private property interests which may have little to
do with what planners would regard as a desirable pattern
of land use. The controls were also characterized by many
detailed regulations which, although they were generally
thought of as health and safety measures, were in fact rather
clumsy means of differentiating between various types and
intensity of land use.

Formidable confusion still exists between the original
functions of control and the objectives set by current concepts of city planning. American planners even now are not
fully convinced that "control" has anything to do with
"planning," and in many city planning departments the two
activities are pursued independently. One reason for this
is that in most cities the controls came before the planning.
In 1953, of the 1,347 cities with over 10,000 population
nearly 800 had enacted comprehensive zoning ordinances
but only 434 had adopted a master plan. The great majority
of these were consultants' plans designed in the 1910–1930
period when the "City Beautiful" movement was in vogue,
and were not intended as guides to the exercise of land-use
control. Zoning developed its own philosophy, but it tended
to emphasize the distinctions between uses rather than the
relationships which tie them together. It is largely for this

reason that many planners regard zoning as more of a hindrance than a help in city planning.

The important question is how far this system of control (rather than the actual controls found in the older types of ordinance) can be adapted to the needs of more purposeful planning policies.

The Objectives of Planning

The federal government's nearest approach to a national policy for urban land use is in the Housing Act of 1949:[1]

The Congress hereby declares that the general welfare and security of the Nation and the health and living standards of its people require housing production and related community development sufficient to remedy the serious housing shortage, the elimination of substandard and other inadequate housing through the clearance of slums and blighted areas, and the realization as soon as feasible of the goal of a decent home and a suitable living environment for every American family.

So far as federal policy is concerned, however, these objectives have been pursued by stimulating the private home-building industry through a very extensive scheme of mortgage insurance and other fiscal techniques. Very little attempt has been made to influence local land-use policies, and what attempt has been made to set standards for private development has been very severely criticized for the low quality and uniformity it encouraged.[2] The urban renewal program, of course, is a remarkable phenomenon. But, despite the encyclopedic instructions issued by the Urban Renewal Administration, very little guidance has been given on the type of land-use controls to be written into a redevelopment contract. Similarly, although up-to-date zoning

1. Compare President Johnson's "Message on the Cities" delivered to Congress on 2nd March 1965. See Part VII.

2. The Department of Housing and Urban Development has been pursuing a far more active policy since its formation in 1965, and is also trying to broaden the basis of local planning. See Part VII.

and subdivision regulations are a requirement of the "workable program" (a standard of city planning activity which is a prerequisite to receiving federal grants for urban renewal), no attempt has been made to revise the Standard Zoning and Subdivision Enabling Acts published in the 1920's or to give other guidance on the administration of land-use control.[3] The related program of federal grants to smaller communities for planning (50 percent of the cost of consultant services) is not accompanied by suggestions as to what the content or objectives of these plans should be.

The scope of planning in America today, therefore, is no wider than the local community's interests. The use made of controls usually reflects local aspirations pretty accurately. The objective may be to boost new tax-producing development. For example, when a new interstate highway branched through an undeveloped corner of a small community near Boston, Massachusetts, the councilmen immediately amended the zoning ordinance to exploit the commercial frontages opened up. Or the objective may be to restrict new residential development to a certain class or character, which led the village of Flower Hill, New York, to require a minimum floor area for new houses of 1,800 square feet. In Carmel, California, which was built as an artists' retreat and is now a very classy seaside resort, the local business community is pressing to have all new commercial sites restricted to 8,000 square feet to protect Carmel's "small town character," or, frankly, to prevent competition with the boutique type of shop which prevails in Carmel.

The most apt summary of American planning policies, whether the objective is to make Dogpatch larger or smaller, is that used by countless mayors in introducing some new plan for downtown or an overdue revision of the zoning ordinance: "TO MAKE FRESNO (or Kalamazoo or wherever) A BETTER PLACE TO LIVE AND DO BUSINESS IN."

3. The American Law Institute is now engaged on a comprehensive review of the law relating to land use, including the preparation of a new Standard Enabling Act. See Part VII.

Planning is so intimately related to local interests that it is difficult to generalize about its objectives. So far as controlling private development is concerned, the job of the planner is largely that of anticipating the trend of private development, making adequate provision for all acceptable uses, and setting standards for new development which reflect local wishes.

America is not deficient in utopian and academic theories of community development, but they tend to be advocated with less conviction than elsewhere. Suggestions for drastically altering the normal trend of development (which inevitably begin by assuming major reform of the governmental structure) are totally unrealistic in the American context. But there is a respectable body of planning philosophy which keeps city planning alive and even influential. The typical statement of a city's planning policies lays much stress on the *efficiency* of the city as a means of communication in the widest sense; its *utility* as a place for the production, exchange, and distribution of goods and services; its *convenience* as a place in which to live and work; and on economy in the *provision* of public services.[4] And it is assumed that these objectives can best be promoted by a strong program of capital investment. American cities tend to have a planning program rather than a planning policy. The emphasis on the programming of public rather than private development is very characteristic of American planning. In a country that has conquered a wilderness in a hundred years, immense importance is attached to the initiative of public authorities in opening up the land with roads, bridges, and basic community facilities. The 41,000-mile federal superhighway program will have a crucial influence on the pattern of future private development.

This report is not concerned with that aspect of land-use planning, but it is very important to remember that in

4. It is comparatively rare to find a city that has tried to state the objectives of its planning policy in more than a cursory manner. The extract from the San Francisco master plan given on pages 146–149 of the appendix expresses typical objectives and principles of American city planning.

America the planning and programming of public works is a major factor influencing private development. In implementing major public policies for community development it is certainly a more important factor than land-use controls.

The New Scope of Control

This does not mean that the scope of the control system is inconsiderable or that the controls themselves are ineffective. In the comprehensive revision of the system now under way or recently completed in most American cities, the trend is to relate the controls more closely to the planning objectives of efficiency and convenience rather than the old objectives of health and safety. This is seen chiefly in the attempt to distinguish more effectively between types of land use and to stress their purpose and location requirements, with far less emphasis on segregation of uses as an end in itself.

The traditional zoning ordinance simply divided the city into three types of use district—residential, commercial and industrial—and established controls over the height and bulk of buildings. This type of ordinance succeeded at least in separating out grossly incompatible uses, holding down the density of residential development, and preventing unhealthy competition for light and air among commercial buildings at the city center. But it was a gross oversimplification, and exceptions had constantly to be made. Also, many aspects of development which required control were outside the scope of the regulations. The result has been, in the last ten years or so, to produce new techniques and revised ordinances which go far beyond the traditional scope of control.

These new controls are described more fully in Part IV, but they can be briefly illustrated by the revised zoning ordinance adopted by Chicago in 1957. Four basic use districts (residence, business, commercial, and manufacturing) were broken down into sixteen major types of activity and further divided into over seventy groups according to building density. The purpose of each of the sixteen major use districts is set down in the ordinance. For example, the following definitions delineate three types of business district:

Local Retail Districts   Local Retail Districts are designed solely for the convenience shopping of persons residing in the adjacent residential areas to permit only such uses as are necessary to satisfy those limited basic shopping needs which occur daily or frequently and so require shopping facilities in close proximity to places of residence.

Restricted Retail Districts   Restricted Retail Districts are designed to cater to the needs of a relatively larger consumer population than served by the Local Retail Districts, and so a wide variety of business uses are permitted for both daily and occasional shopping.

General Retail Districts   General Retail Districts are designed to cater to the needs of a larger consumer population than that served by Restricted Retail Districts and so are mapped typically in major shopping center locations characterized by large establishments generating larger volumes of vehicular and pedestrian traffic.

There are four other types of business district, four types of commercial district, and three manufacturing. When this degree of use districting is reached, the planner has a reasonably effective and precise tool for planning the use of land and controlling the standards of development. In addition, the ordinance distinguishes between types of industrial use by defining highly technical "performance standards" covering noise, vibration, smell, smoke, fire, and explosive hazards and glare or heat. It also specifies the off-street parking and loading requirements for all uses. It controls the height and bulk of buildings by a flexible floor area ratio device, and sets standards for the layout and density of residential areas. Detailed controls over signs and billboards are introduced. It deals with nonconforming uses by setting an amortization period within which they must be ended. Finally, it distinguishes a large number of "special uses" which cannot be logically restricted to any one district, and which require the specific consent of the zoning authority.

In these revised systems, use districting remains the basic control but the new techniques define land uses more accurately and also take account of the relationships among uses. This is leading in some communities to a much finer adjustment of the controls to neighborhood characteristics, rather than generalized use districts with uniform standards. There is no doubt that the more precise the planners can be in stating their objectives, the more relevant and effective the controls can be.

The Ideology

The objectives of the American system of land-use control are to mitigate the effects of growth and change and set standards of new development. Where development creates conflicts of interest in a community, then control is warranted. But the process of expansion or change is not to be radically redirected. This view does not derive simply from the dogma of private enterprise. It is also grounded in a belief that the development of cities is shaped by influences too powerful or too complex to be controlled. Therefore control is best directed at promoting a healthy environment, while not restricting private initiative or removing the profit motive from development. The controls are adapted to the natural process of growth, rather than made powerful enough to alter that process radically. The exercise of control then requires a rather nice adjustment of means to ends.

The objectives and methods of American planning might be summarized as follows:

1. Preventing conflicts of private interest in land use (zoning).

2. Preventing conflicts of private and public interest in land use (master planning).

3. Preventing conflicts of various public interests (master planning and capital investment programming).

4. Securing sound standards of new development (zoning and subdivision regulation).

5. Facilitating private development and encouraging private investment (the whole planning process, including urban renewal).

6. Making Our Town a better place to live and do business in—efficiency, convenience, and economy are the criteria.

IV METHODS

The revised (1960) zoning ordinance of New York runs to 300,000 words. Some other major cities have adopted regulations almost as long and every bit as complicated. The only way to get acquainted with the character and scope of these controls is to read a few examples. This chapter briefly describes some of the more important new techniques.

The basic Amercian methods of land-use control are zoning and subdivision regulation. Zoning is the division of jurisdiction into districts ("zones") within which permissible uses are prescribed and restrictions on building height, bulk, layout, and other requirements are defined. The regulations are uniform in all districts zoned for the same use. Subdivision regulations specify minimum standards that apply to all new residential development: street design and construction, the arrangement of lots, drainage, water supply, sewerage, and in some cases street signs, tree planting, fire hydrants, street lighting, etc. Subdivision control may also be used to secure other objectives, such as provision of parks and school sites, and to regulate the pace and location of new development. There are also fire, housing, and building codes that regulate the safety, health, and construction standards of new development, and that apply uniformly to the city or other governmental unit. There is also a power, rarely used, to prepare an official street map. This establishes the legal status of existing and proposed streets, and after its adoption any new building erected in the line of a proposed street can be removed without compensation. No compensation is payable to property owners adversely affected by any of these regulations, but provision is made for administrative or legislative review on appeal and all such actions are subject to judicial review.

The controls are established under the police power of the states, as delegated to cities and counties. The enabling legislature differs from state to state. So do decisions on

41

land-use controls by the state courts. Each town, city, or county writes its own regulations, and these range from the most rudimentary (or in many cases none at all) to the most complex and sophisticated, while the quality and consistency of their administration varies almost as widely.

One of the values of the American system of land-use control is that it admits variety and allows experiment. But by the same token it is virtually impossible to describe the system thoroughly. In recent years many ingenious and effective innovations have been introduced in individual cities which may go completely unnoticed outside that locality, except perhaps in some obscure law journal. But it is chiefly in these innovations that the interest of the American system lies. Zoning and controls similar to subdivision regulation have been employed by most European countries. Zoning originated in Germany in the 1880's, and planning schemes under the British Planning Act of 1932 usually included this type of control. But since the war most European countries, under the pressure of reconstruction, have relied more on direct governmental control of development and less on the formalized systems of control. Probably none has gone so far as Britain in abandoning written standards and relying on discretionary control under the general guidance of a development plan. The United States, however, is the one country where the traditional system remains unimpaired, and it is interesting to see the efforts being made to adapt it to the conditions of modern development and the needs of more positive planning policies. The bulk of this chapter is devoted to describing the more important and promising of these innovations.

Zoning

The most significant trends in the current revision of the zoning system are (1) an attempt to relate controls more closely to planning criteria, and (2) an attempt to make controls more flexible without greatly extending the discretionary power of the planning authority.

Density Regulations

The traditional zoning ordinance includes detailed "dimensional" controls that specify the height (in feet and/or stories), minimum depth of side, front and back yards, minimum lot size, and frontage, and percentage of the lot to be left unbuilt upon. The standards vary according to the use district. Most modern ordinances retain most of these controls, especially in low-density residential areas, but it is now customary to allow greater latitude in design and layout by introducing the floor area ratio device.[1] Some cities have tried to tackle the problem of residential density more directly by specifying the number of persons, families, or dwelling units per acre. None that I know of (except New York) has used the more accurate and flexible standard of habitable rooms or bedspaces per acre. In general, despite (or because of) their particularity, these controls are not very satisfactory. Builders almost invariably adopt the minimum standards. This results in gross uniformity and, since the current vogue is for the sixty-foot "ranch" house with a two-car garage on a hundred-foot frontage, the appearance of overcrowding. The floor area ratio system does not assure the generous open space that it theoretically permits. Detailed controls appropriate to the development of a one-house plot can hopelessly impede a more subtle relationship between buildings in a large-scale development.

To overcome these disadvantages, the revised New York ordinance introduces a string of new devices which make the calculation of permitted density a mathematical feat. Ten types of residential district are defined according to building type and permitted density. The traditional dimensional controls are retained for lot size and frontage in districts of single and semidetached ("duplex") houses, and the number of dwelling units per acre is specified. In all other districts density is controlled by specifying maximum rooms per acre and minimum lot area per room. Building height, bulk, open space, and space between buildings are also con-

1. I.e., the ratio between the total floor area of the building (excluding shafts, etc.) and the ground area of the site.

trolled. Height and building setback are regulated first by specific dimensional controls in both residential and commercial districts, and also by a control called a "sky exposure plane" which relates permissible height to a setback at the upper stories. Building bulk is controlled by floor area ratio standards, but since this would permit developers to cover the whole site with a low building, the regulations also contain a novel "open space-area ratio" which expresses the amount of open space that must be provided on a lot as a percentage not of the lot but of the floor area of the proposed building, i.e.:

$$\frac{\text{Open space} \times 100}{\text{Floor area}} \cdot$$

The open space must be available to all occupants of the building, but half of it may be used for off-street parking. Another novel formula provides an alternative to standard specifications for space between buildings in the case of a large-scale development (e.g., several high-rise apartment blocks). This is

$$S = \frac{2(HA + HB) + LA + LB}{6}$$

where

S = Required minimum spacing between a wall of building A and a wall of building B

HA = Height of building A

HB = Height of building B

LA = Length of that part of building A directly opposite building B

LB = Length of that part of building B directly opposite building A

For example, if the length of the parts of the two buildings directly opposite each other is 60 feet, and building A is 100 feet high and building B is 140 feet high, the required distance between buildings would be

$$\frac{2(100 + 140) + 60 + 60,}{6}$$, or a distance of 100 feet.

I have no idea whether such a formula would ensure a satisfactory layout, but it certainly allows greater flexibility.

Perhaps the most attractive innovation is a provision that allows a "bonus" in permitted height and bulk when the developer devotes more land than is strictly required to open space. In the downtown apartment districts and commercial zones, bonuses are provided for plazas and arcades. It is hoped that this will encourage tall slim buildings, like Lever Brothers and Seagram on Park Avenue, over the squat "wedding cake" architecture which the old controls favored.

The New York ordinance combines all these controls, the traditional and the new, in a highly subtle manner to provide a wide range of building type and density, and if the architects and their clients will accept it, ample opportunity for variety in design, besides new open space at the sidewalk level. The details of these controls, however, are less significant than the planning authority's claim that residential density standards have been related not to vague generalizations about types of residential neighborhood but to the "capacity" of a district in terms of public transport, roads, schools, open space, and other community facilities. Whether or not these criteria have actually been followed in the present revision, the principle is clearly valid and must eventually replace the old subjective values on which so-called density regulations have been based.

Use Regulations

All the controls included in zoning regulations are really means of defining types and intensity of land use. The most important improvements in the zoning system have been to define types of use district more precisely, to take account of the relationships between uses, and to assess the location requirements of particular uses as well as the conflicts between uses. These refinements are important because the American zoning system does not allow latitude in the use districts. They are not (as in the British development plans) "primarily" residential or "primarily" commercial zones; instead the ordinance must state precisely what uses are allowed in each use district. In the past this problem has often been met by making frequent amendments (i.e. exceptions to the zoning regulations). Some of the best new ordinances meet this need by defining many more use zones than the old single-family residence, general residence, commercial, and industrial districts. The new (1957) Chicago ordinance has sixteen major use districts and over seventy subdistricts, each with a distinct character based on building density. The revised New York ordinance provides for thirteen major districts, the Santa Clara County ordinance (1959) defines twenty, the Washington D. C. ordinance (1958) eighteen. This is a much more detailed breakdown of private land use (excluding private open space, which is not shown in American zoning ordinances) than is usually given in British development plans.

In most ordinances the purpose of these districts is left implicit in the regulations, but a few cities have tried to state the intention explicitly, and this certainly assists in judging the reasonableness and utility of the controls. The Washington D. C. ordinance, for example, explains the purpose of separate residential districts:

R.1. Districts (One-family detached dwellings) This district is designed to protect quiet residential areas now developed with one-family detached dwellings and adjoining vacant areas likely to be developed for such purposes.
The regulations are designed to stabilize such areas and to promote a suitable environment for family life. For that reason only a few additional and compatible uses are permitted.

R.4. Districts (Row houses, conversions, and apartments) These districts are designed to include those areas now developed primarily with row (terrace) houses, but within which there have been a substantial number of conversions of such dwellings into dwellings for two or more families. Very little vacant land would be included within this district since its primary purpose would be the stabilization of remaining one-family dwellings. Since much of this district would lie within urban renewal areas, the demolition of substandard structures and replacement with low-density apartment houses (flats) should be encouraged.

R.5. Districts (General Residence Districts) These districts are intended to permit a flexibility of design by permitting in a single district all types of urban residential development provided they comply with the height, density, and area requirements established for residential districts.

The British planner would probably say "Let the whole place be 'general residence,'" but the more exclusive zones do reflect very marked preferences held by the American homeowner.

Each use zone lists in detail all the uses permitted in that zone and in many cases the precise intensity and character of use (e.g., the maximum number of employees, type of equipment, etc.) and the conditions under which such uses are allowed. An example from the San Francisco zoning ordinance is given on pages 150–151 of the appendix; this is the second of three commercial zones in the San Francisco zoning ordinance: this zone also allows any type of residential development and all the uses permitted in the first commercial zone.

It is the listing of permitted uses that makes the modern zoning ordinance so lengthy, and there is always the problem of the novel use or combination of uses which is not specifically listed. When motels first appeared in the United States, they were forced into the all-purpose industrial districts because they were not listed as a permitted use elsewhere. The New York ordinance introduces an excellent device for simplifying the listing of permitted uses while employing a wide range of use districts. It first establishes thirteen major use districts and states their purpose in fairly specific terms (see pages 152–155). It also defines eighteen "use groups" which describe in general terms the principal types of activity or development (see pages 156–158). Finally, an index lists 425 different uses and shows to which use group they belong. The ordinance then states which use groups are permitted in each district (see table on page 159). As new uses appear an official determination is made to decide in which use group they belong. The use districts are further distinguished by the density controls already described. By varying the combination of use groups in each district, a generous range of neighborhood types can be provided for, and by careful analysis of neighborhood needs and characteristics it is possible to plan an economic and convenient arrangement of uses.

The British planner, with his broad use categories and ad hoc control, may brush all this aside as impossibly cumbersome. But where the legal framework requires absolute consistency and public opinion demands the minimum discretionary power in the hands of local officials, planning has to be systematic. The ingenuity of American planners and their legal draftsmen in securing flexibility within these limits is rather admirable.

Performance Standards

A few years ago, dissatisfaction with the rigidity of traditional use zones led to the suggestion that control should be related not to *use* but to *effect*. If an industry could meet certain very high standards of operation and appearance, there was no reason why it should not be allowed in residential areas, where it might be more convenient to the employees' homes. The problem then became one of establishing technical "performance standards." Most zoning controls (height, bulk, density, etc.) are in effect performance standards, or, conversely, performance standards are improved ways of distinguishing between different types of use.

Performance standards have been developed to deal with the following types of potential nuisance: noise, vibration, smoke, dust and other particulate matter, odor, toxic, and noxious matter, fire and explosive hazards, humidity, heat and glare, and radiation hazards. The standards are highly technical, and there is no point in setting them out in detail in this report. The most thoroughgoing examples are in the Chicago and New York ordinances; the New York provisions governing noise are reproduced on pages 160–162.

No city has been bold enough to abandon traditional use district boundaries, but several have adopted performance standards to provide a higher degree of differentiation among industrial zones and to map out the least noxious of these close to residential districts.

The American Society of Planning Officials has reported that over 200 zoning ordinances now employ performance standards. So far these standards have not been reviewed in the courts, and both their efficacy and equity are an open question. Some major cities have decided to omit them from current zoning revisions because they have yet to be proved. The chief difficulty seen is not in the preparation of scientific standards but in their administration. They go far beyond the normal competence of a zoning enforcement officer. Some cities have met this problem by submitting all such cases to a private consultant and requiring the developer to pay the fees. Nevertheless, it is the prime example of the American attempt to control land uses by specific standards.

Other Zoning Methods of Use Control

Some land uses are not amenable to the grouping of uses in generalized use zones: they may be perfectly acceptable in certain locations within a district but not in others, or they may be acceptable only if certain features are more closely controlled than the zoning ordinance allows, or they may be uses which are acceptable in any zone provided they are on a large enough site, or they may be acceptable uses whose actual location is impossible to predict. Three devices are now in use to deal with these problems: the special-use zone, the special-use permit or conditional use, and the so-called "floating zone."

1. The Special-Use Zone. This device provides a separate use zone for one particular use or small group of closely related uses. It is a return to the very early days of zoning, when Los Angeles (around 1910) adopted funeral parlor districts, cow districts, motion picture districts, billboard districts, and so forth. Recently the device has been revived: Tucson, Arizona, has a mobile home zone; Phoenix, Arizona, has a parking lot zone and a zone for multiple-story garages; Santa Clara County, California, has a professional office zone (see pages 163–164).

The city of Oakland, California (population about 400,-000), has developed a variation of the special use district, which they call the "combination zone." This is a separate parcel of controls, more specific than those in the general use districts, which can be added to any use zone or group of zones in a particular neighborhood. The purpose of this is to allow certain types of use in some, but not all, areas of the same general use zone. For example, instead of allowing motels in all residential and commercial districts, it is possible to combine the motel zone with certain districts at the most convenient locations: see pages 165–167. The advantage of this over a special-use zone is that a special-use zone would have either to exclude or include these other types of use, whereas the combination zone allows these uses to combine with motels only where this combination is appropriate. It is a sound device which facilitates accurate land-use planning.

2. *The Special-Use Permit or Conditional Use.* Most of the newer ordinances list the uses which are permitted "as of right" in each zone, and also list "special" or "conditional" uses which may be permitted upon the approval of the planning authority after a report by the planning director and a public hearing. There has been much criticism of this device, since it obviously runs counter to the principle that zoning is a specific, not a discretionary, form of control. The Chicago ordinance, for example, makes the following uses subject to special permits in Local Retail Districts:

1. Airports, or aircraft landing fields, and heliports
2. Churches
3. Convents, monasteries, rectories, parish houses
4. Government-operated health centers
5. Hospitals and sanitariums

6. Municipal or privately owned recreation buildings or community centers
7. Parking lots or garages, other than accessory, for the storage of motor vehicles under 1½ ton capacity
8. Parks and playgrounds
9. Penal and correctional institutions
10. Public utility and public service uses, including:
    (a) Bus terminals, turnarounds (off street), bus garages, bus lots, street railway terminals, or streetcar houses
    (b) Electric substations
    (c) Fire stations
    (d) Police stations
    (e) Public art galleries and museums
    (f) Public libraries
    (g) Railroad passenger stations
    (h) Railroad rights-of-way
    (i) Telephone exchanges, microwave relay towers, and telephone transmission eqiupment buildings
    (j) Water filtration plants
    (k) Water pumping stations
    (l) Water reservoirs
11. Radio and television towers
12. Stadiums, auditoriums, and arenas

The inclusion of various public uses is unconventional, since zoning control normally applies only to private development. The special permit procedure brings such public uses under surveillance of the planning authority, but its decision does not necessarily prevail over that of another public body. The main objection to the special-use permit is that it subjects private development to control without specifying standards which it must meet or by which the fairness of the planning authority's decision can be judged. A few ordinances now state the general terms on which special permits may be granted. For example, the proposed Boston ordinance states that

The Board of Appeals shall approve any such application only if it finds that in its judgment all the following conditions are met:

1. the specific site is an appropriate location for such a use;
2. the use as developed will not adversely affect the neighborhood;
3. there will be no nuisance or serious hazard to vehicles or pedestrians;
4. adequate and appropriate facilities will be provided for the proper operation of the proposed use.

But it goes on to give the Board wide powers to make its approval subject to conditions:

In approving a conditional use, the Board may attach such conditions and safeguards as are deemed necessary to protect the neighborhood, such as but not limited to the following:

1. requirement of front, side, or rear yards, greater than the minimum required by this Code;
2. requirement of screening of parking areas or other parts of the premises from adjoining premises or from the street, by walls, fences, planting, or other devices, as specified by the Board of Appeals:
3. modification of the exterior features or appearance of the structure;
4. limitation of size, number of occupants, method or time of operation, or extent of facilities;
5. regulation of number, design, and location requirement of off-street parking or other special features beyond the minimum required by this or other applicable codes or regulations.

Such innovations move toward the British system of discretionary control, and there was a time about five years ago when the tendency was given a cautious welcome. But the American distrust of political control and distaste for bureaucratic power has led to renewed insistence on specific standards for special exceptions and conditional uses. The New York ordinance does attempt to set down for each category of special use the findings of fact which the Board of Appeals must make and the conditions with which the proposed development must comply: an example is the standard for permitting gasoline stations in certain commercial districts given on pages 168–169.

3. *The "Floating Zone."* This can best be described as a combination of the special-use district and the special-use permit procedure. A special-use district is defined but is not applied to any particular area until a developer asks the planning authority to rezone his land in that category. The standards established for such a zone include the minimum area (usually several acres) to which such a zone can be applied. The device was originated in Tarrytown, New York (and upheld by the courts), where a new zone was established in which lots of not less than ten acres could be used for mixed residential development (flats and single homes) provided only 15 percent of the total area was built upon. The advantage of such a system is that the planning authority sets the standards for a certain type of development but leaves the actual location of such uses to private initiative. This is particularly useful when the use involved has no nuisance factor, or when the nuisance factors can be mitigated by spacious surroundings, and when the location requirements are so flexible that precise districts cannot reasonably be planned in advance. An example of this device is the proposed floating zone for row houses (terrace housing) in El Paso, Texas—pages 170–171. The same technique could perhaps be used to control the large-scale shopping center development, which seems to locate almost anywhere but needs to be carefully controlled.

In undeveloped areas the floating zone avoids the invidious task of assigning high commercial values to certain sites and denying them to others. The market then makes the decisions. This may not result in good overall planning but, where there is no power to pay compensation for denying development value, the market is at least an impartial adjudicator and the zoning controls ensure that the essential public interests are safeguarded.

Planned Developments

One of the main disadvantages of traditional zoning regulations has been that they were geared to the normal process of piecemeal development on individual lots. They often proved a severe handicap in planning the use and layout of a large-scale development. The arrangement and size of buildings were tied to artificial boundary lines, and highly desirable subsidiary uses (e.g. local retail stores, personal services, and communal laundries) were prohibited by the use zoning. Several recent zoning ordinances (New York, Washington, D. C., and San Francisco among others) have provided what amounts to a "floating zone" for large-scale developments. Height, bulk, and open space regulations are relaxed to allow varied layout and provision is made for local shopping and services in scale with proposed residential development. Planned shopping centers or other major commercial or office developments may be dealt with in a similar way. In most cases the ordinances do not go into great detail about the requirements for such planned developments. They specify the minimum area (usually ten acres or more), require the submission of plans, and leave a wide latitude for negotiation with the developer. This is sensible since the type of developer in mind here may be expected to employ a competent designer, and the aim is to allow scope for fresh ideas. The San Francisco "planned unit development" controls are given on pages 172–173.[2]

Neighborhood Standards

Another aspect of the current attempt to escape from the oversimplified and too uniform controls of traditional zoning is the tendency in some cities to create use zones which are adapted to only one or two neighborhoods. One reason for this practice is that with changing social conditions and living habits some of the older residential areas find that traditional controls are not adequate to prevent deterioration: incongruous or poor quality new development, overcrowding and overbuilding permitted by too generous controls, and other blighting influences may be at work. Alternatively, the aim may be to foster or retain the identity

2. See also the account of more recent provisions for "unit" or "cluster" residential developments in Part VII.

of neighborhoods with a more limited range of use or more precise character than that implied by the general use zones. For example, the New Haven, Connecticut, ordinance provides a series of nine different residential zones, the more recent of which are attempts to protect particular neighborhoods; for example:

Residence "AAA" Districts
This district exists for the protection of certain multifamily areas of relatively small total size but of unique and irreplaceable value to the community as a whole. The specific purpose of this district is to stabilize and preserve the existing residential character of these areas to the maximum possible extent. To this end the use of land and buildings within these areas is limited primarily to relatively high density residential uses, as the particular character, size and surroundings of these areas create little need for the location within their boundaries of further such non-residential uses as generally support a residential area. Moreover, these areas are found especially along major streets traversing large residential sections of the City, and the outward movement of streets would constitute a serious threat to the residential quality of the areas to either side of them. Encroachment of office or other commercial uses along these streets would violate the spirit of this ordinance and its general purpose and intent and, any other provision of this ordinance to the contrary notwithstanding, no variance shall be granted for such uses in this district. It is hereby found and declared that these regulations are necessary to the protection of these areas and that their protection is essential to the maintenance of a balanced community of sound residential areas of diverse types.

Another recent example comes from Oakland, California. The city contains one of the largest private medical centers in the western states—a group of three private hospitals surrounded by the homes and offices of several hundred doctors, dentists, and other medical specialists. At the request of the medical community, the city planning department recently studied ways of arresting incipient deterioration in the area and ensuring its future well-being as a medical center. The planners came up with many suggestions, some of which depended on private initiative and some of which could be acted on by the city. These included a special use zone which restricted the neighborhood to all types of medical use—clinics, hospitals, research laboratories, etc.; all types of residential use, including homes for nurses; and, as conditional uses, certain service establishments for patients, doctors, or medical center employees. The detailed use regulations are given on pages 174–175; further controls govern height and density, and parking requirements for each type of use.

This conception of devising controls to fit the needs of particular neighborhoods seems a distinct improvement over the old method of establishing general use zones and then applying them with a broad brush to existing neighborhoods. Its success depends, of course, on the thoroughness and skill with which neighborhoods are defined and their needs analyzed. A concern for neighborhood values is perhaps a sign of a more mature and humane approach to landuse control. Its origin in those cities which are developing it can probably be traced to experience in the rehabilitation work of urban renewal.

Other Types of Zoning Control

1. *Miscellaneous Controls.* One of the more dubious advantages of a zoning ordinance is that it can be used as a ragbag for all sorts of regulations which overload the landuse control system and could be better dealt with by local bylaws or tenancy agreements and restrictive covenants. The zoning ordinance of Freemont, California, includes the following as an "accessory use" in residential zones:

(e) Keeping of not to exceed an aggregate of five (5) cats or dogs over ten (10) weeks in age and/or ten (10) chickens, not including roosters, for each dwelling unit.

Some other miscellaneous controls, however, do require the districting structure which the zoning ordinance provides, and are properly conditions of land use. The obvious examples are the off-street parking and loading facilities which are a feature in all modern zoning ordinances. The New York ordinance sets out in immense detail the minimum, and in some cases the maximum, parking space required for all types of development and provides sliding scales to match varying factors such as residents, visitors, customers, employees, etc. Hotels, for example, must provide X parking spaces per X guest rooms, and in addition X spaces in relation to the floor area capacity used for banquet halls, conference rooms, dining rooms and bars, wedding chapels, and television studios. The ordinance even specifies the parking requirements for tennis courts, churches, and prisons.

2. *Special-Purpose Zones.* The districting device also lends itself to creation of special zones—for example, to limit building height around airports or to protect watershed areas. The Federal Flood Insurance Act of 1956 requires local authorities to zone areas subject to flooding as a condition of participating in the scheme. The only drawback to including these zones in the land-use control system is that they are usually much larger than the use zones and have to be superimposed on the use-zone structure. But they are clearly factors affecting land-use planning, and it is often convenient to include them in the control system.

3. *Agriculture and Forestry Zones.* It seems reasonable to assume that if land-use controls are a legitimate means of protecting residential zones and avoiding conflicts arising from different types of urban land use, then the same principles will support the use of control to protect rural values and to mitigate the conflicts that arise where urban uses impinge on established agricultural interests. The use of zoning to promote sound agricultural land use and discourage uneconomic agricultural settlement seems to have been fairly effective in the few states where it has been practiced. Wisconsin and a few neighboring states have used rural zoning since the 1930's to assist reforestation and to prevent settlement of subarable lands.

It is only quite recently, however, that there has been an

attempt to extend zoning controls to protect productive agricultural land from the threat of suburbanization. There is so much agricultural land in America, and the problem of surplus crops is so intractable, that there is generally no incentive to keep farmland free from development. In a few areas, however, the productive value of orchards and market gardens is so great that the farming community welcomes the protection afforded by zoning. The idea started in Santa Clara County, California, which contains some of the finest fruit farms in the world, including a thousand-acre pear farm. The county produces cherries, apricots, peaches, strawberries, walnuts, and plums, besides vast quantities of salad crops. And yet in the past fifteen years thousands of acres of these irreplaceable orchards have been bulldozed for suburban housing. Lying at the foot of the San Francisco Bay area it is the second fastest growing region in the United States. Even those farmers who resist selling out at inflated values may be forced to capitulate as they find their land being surrounded by suburban development and deteriorating as trespassing and air pollution increase. Moreover, tax assessment laws require land to be assessed not for its existing use but for its fair market value, and the farmer cannot afford to farm land assessed at residential values. The fact that even if land is zoned for agricultural use it may still be taxed for its speculative value is the biggest anomaly in American land-use planning. The constitutional provision which requires land to be taxed at fair market value, which was originally intended to avoid penal or discriminatory tax assessments, now results in exactly what it was designed to prevent. But the assessor can fairly claim that use zoning has been known to change as speculative values increase. It is a problem which may only be solved when there is greater confidence in the permanence of agricultural use zoning.

Santa Clara and some other counties have introduced special use districts for agricultural land which restrict it to all types of farming and related uses (see pages 176–177). A statement of policy for these areas by the County Planning Commission and Board of Supervisors (the elected body) is given on page 178–179. A distinctive feature of the Santa Clara County system is that land can be zoned for agriculture only if the farmer requests it; but already several thousand acres have been zoned, ranging from the 100-acre Kadjevich orchards to the 4,870 acres of the Berryessa mixed farm. No minimum area is specified, but the policy is to encourage zones of at least 100 acres. The larger the groups of contiguous zones, the less conflict arises with suburban development, and the more likely it is that tax assessments will reflect the dominant agricultural use.

Those who believe in the importance of agricultural zoning have had a tough job to get it started, and there seems little likelihood that it will be widely adopted or prove a means of saving agricultural land for its recreational and landscape value. But the validity of the method is clear and its benefits should become apparent. It is not the system but the demand for it that is lacking.

4. *Aesthetic and Historic Zoning.* Generally speaking, American planning controls stop short of any attempt at architectural control. Layout is certainly influenced by subdivision regulations and density controls, but there is rarely any control over building design or materials. The courts have consistently discouraged such attempts, and the only area in which aesthetic considerations have been allowed to enter explicitly into the planning process is in the control of billboards. In 1935 the Massachusetts Supreme Court disposed of fifteen cases concerning control of advertisements which had been in litigation for ten years. The decision supported the abolition of billboards from areas of historic interest and landscape value, and also upheld the control of size, location, and design in other areas. Among the signs banished was a huge Chevrolet roof sign overlooking Boston Common and the State House. The court remarked that "Considerations of taste and fitness may be a proper basis for action in granting or denying permits for advertising devices."

In 1954 the U.S. Supreme Court in a famous judgment on an urban renewal case (*Berman* v. *Parker*) held that "It is within the power of the legislature to determine that the community should be beautiful as well as healthy, spacious as well as clean, well-balanced as well as carefully patrolled." This was widely interpreted as an endorsement of aesthetic controls and has led to a splurge of new regulations conferring wide powers on planning commissions to control the design and appearance of new development. But in *Berman* v. *Parker* it was the exercise of the power of eminent domain, under which compensation is paid for injury to private interests, that was at issue—not the police power, under which land-use controls are exercised and which carries no compensation. The distinction is vital, and it is doubtful whether the new controls will survive the scrutiny of the courts, since they generally involve a discretionary power of "architectural review" quite at odds with the traditional pattern of development control in America.

Nor do the aesthetic controls that have been developed inspire much confidence. A comprehensive survey of the subject, with copious examples of the controls now in use, is in a report, "Planning and Community Appearance," published by the New York chapters of the American Institute of Architects and the American Institute of Planners in 1958. The report cites examples from some thirty or forty communities which have experimented with aesthetic control. Some of them are quite ludicrous, such as the "no-look-alike" and "must-look-alike" regulations which attempt to enforce or prohibit variety, and those which speak in terms of style, such as the comic-opera zoning ordinance of Coral Gables, Florida, which requires that "all buildings shall be Spanish, Venetian, Italian, or other Mediterranean or similar harmonious type architecture."

But such attempts are very exceptional, and it must be admitted that they do often secure a degree of coherence and conformity in a community which is rather delightful in America because it is so rare. Coming into Santa Barbara, California, one is immediately struck by the cohesion of style and the absence of the usual crudities of downtown. In fact, almost the whole city was rebuilt after the earthquake of 1925, and an architectural Board of Review enforced compliance with the "Monterey" style through the issue of over 2,000 building permits in eight months. The result is one of the most attractive towns in America.

The most successful and least meretricious aesthetic controls are those designed to protect a specific area of historic, architectural, scenic, or civic importance. There are many of these, including the areas surrounding most state capitals, and historic sites in Concord, Lexington, and Salem, Massachusetts; Charleston, South Carolina; Natchez, Mississippi; and Williamsburg, Virginia. The regulations usually require submission of all proposals for new development to a Board of Architectural Review, which has power to withhold approval or enforce modifications in design. Some, such as the very successful Vieux Carré Commission in New Orleans, also exercise control over demolition, alterations, repairs, and accessory development such as signs and redecoration. By a recent addition to its powers, the Vieux Carré Commission can enforce the repair and proper maintenance of historic buildings in private ownership (see pages 180–181).

In all these cases, control is limited to areas of acknowledged importance, either the whole of a small community or a strategic area in a larger city. The advantage of such a limitation is that both the aptness of the control exercised and its effects can be readily seen and assessed. It need not be restricted to measures of preservation or enforce compliance with a notional style, but it can limit public control to those areas for which genuine public concern is felt. It avoids the inevitably futile attempt to improve the general standard of taste by coercion, which would in any case outrage the average American's ideas of personal liberty and the proper place of government.

Nonconforming Uses

In theory a zoning ordinance applies to both existing and new development and is therefore retroactive, but most zoning ordinances have a saving clause which permits the continuance of existing uses that are nonconforming either as to use or detailed requirements. In an early test case the California supreme court upheld a city's right to force a brick works out of a residential zone, even though the brick works had been in the area long before it was developed for residential use. But the inequity of such a procedure, where no compensation was payable, appears to have prevented any general enforcement of this kind. Later ordinances often provided that nonconforming buildings could not be extended or rebuilt, nor one nonconforming use be replaced by another, nor resumed after a certain lapse of time.

Recently, several major cities have decided to tackle this problem in a more methodical and discriminating manner. Nonconformance is broken down into various classes, for example:

1. Nonconforming use of open land—junk yard of used car lot.
2. Nonconforming signs, advertisements, and similar light structures.
3. Nonconforming use of a nonconforming building—a small shop in a house in a residential district.
4. Nonconforming use of a building specifically designed for that purpose—a factory in a residential district.
5. Buildings conforming as to use but not in conformance with dimensional or other requirements of a physical character.

Each of these categories presents different degrees of nuisance and investment, and removal would be far less of a hardship in some cases than in others. Buildings in class 5 are usually allowed to continue if it is impractical to alter them to meet the new requirements. For the other types of nonconforming use it is now common to set an amortization period with which the use must be ended or removed to an appropriate district. No compensation is paid but the amortization period supposedly bears some relation to the economic life of the structure. Meanwhile it enjoys a monopolistic position by being located in an area from which competitors are excluded (which may help commercial uses and advertisements but is of little value to industrial and other uses).

The New York ordinance confines the amortization device to nonconforming uses in residential areas as follows:

Nonconforming Use	Amortization Period
Industrial uses in non-residential buildings	25–40 years
Specified objectionable uses (junkyards, coal yards, etc.)	10 years
Industrial uses in residential buildings	10 years
Open uses and advertisements (small investments)	3 years

Baltimore, in April 1955, passed an ordinance requiring all billboards and similar advertisements to be removed from residential areas within five years; by April 1960, the removal was complete. The city now proposes to apply a similar provision to nonconforming open land uses (junkyards, etc.) which requires their removal from residential and office districts within three years.

The Chicago ordinance sets an amortization period of five years for nonconforming buildings of less than $2,000 valuation, and ten years for buildings of $2,000–5,000 valuation (with certain exceptions in commercial districts). Nonconforming uses of residential buildings in a residential district have to be discontinued in eight or fifteen years according to the type of use. Buildings designed for business use but in use for commercial or industrial purposes must cease to be so used within fifteen years. Nonconforming use of land without buildings must be discontinued within five years. Chicago also has a unique provision allowing the city to end certain nonconforming uses at an earlier date by compulsorily acquiring them under the power of eminent domain.

The new San Francisco ordinance is more cautious and sets amortization periods (five years) only for nonconforming open land uses, commercial and industrial buildings valued at less than $500, and billboards—with the characteristic zoning quibble that if the billboard is located within 250 feet of a commercial or manufacturing district, or if the lot on which it stands is "landscaped" (defined as "at least the planting of a suitable ground cover between the sign . . . and the front lot line") within one year from the date of the ordinance, then it can continue for not more than twenty years.

The New York ordinance deals with nonconforming industrial uses in industrial or commercial zones by requiring that they meet certain performance standards within fifteen years. Other ordinances set varying restrictions on the continuance of nonconforming uses according to the character of the use and its relation to other uses.

One difficulty in regulating nonconforming uses is to establish which uses were legally existing at the time of the ordinance, and those which appear subsequently and do not therefore qualify for the exemptions granted by the ordinance. To meet this some cities require registration of all nonconforming uses, sometimes with reregistration on an annual or periodic basis.

There is as yet little experience of the amortization device since the periods set for the more valuable uses will not expire for many years. But in 1954 the California Court of Appeals upheld a five-year amortization period set by Los Angeles for the commercial or industrial use of a residential building in a residential district. The unequivocal tone of this decision has given encouragement to other cities, but similar cases elsewhere have met with mixed judgments and decisions have been based on the merits of the case rather than on the principle involved. There are a good many pitfalls, notably the differences among amortization periods for similar uses in different cities, and the allowance of some nonconforming uses but not others. This practice may fall foul of the constitutional requirement of "equal protection." Nevertheless, the attempt to deal with the backlog of nonconforming uses, which traditional zoning left untouched, is one of the boldest innovations of recent years and shows that some American cities, at least, are prepared to use stern measures in the effort to control land use.

Administration

The four main aspects of zoning administration are the day-to-day enforcement of controls, the hearing of appeals for special exceptions to be made in individual cases, the procedure for amending the regulations or the district boundaries shown on the zoning map, and the scope for judicial review of administrative action.

1. *Enforcement.* The original zoning ordinance is prepared by the city planning department or by consultants. After approval of the ordinance by the planning commission (a nonelected body) and adoption by the city council (or county supervisors or selectmen), administration is usually vested not in the planning department but in the building inspector. The building inspector, in enforcing the code, issues permits which are necessary before construction can begin and also use permits which are required before the finished building can be occupied. The procedure provides a convenient hook on which to hang zoning enforcement, and most ordinances simply provide that the building inspector cannot issue permits unless the proposed development complies with the zoning regulations.

Building inspection and land-use control do not have a great deal in common, however, and as more complex zoning controls, based on more subtle planning concepts, have developed, some cities have appointed "zoning administrators" who usually have a professional planning background. All applications for building permits are referred to the zoning administrator, and his certificate of compliance is required before the building inspector may issue a permit. It may sound somewhat Parkinsonian, but it makes for more competent and consistent administration of the zoning controls.

None of these officials, however, may use his discretion in allowing variation in the literal application of the controls, however slight, or in permitting exceptions in cases of special hardship or other extenuating circumstances. One or two cities have entrusted the zoning administrator with power to grant certain minor variations in the dimensional controls but only within limits specified in the ordinance. These functions are customarily handled by a specially constituted Board of Appeals or Board of Adjustment.

2. *Appeals.* The Board of Appeals is usually a quasi-independent body appointed by the mayor, but may also be a committee of the city council. It generally consists of some five members serving overlapping three- or four-year terms; members are usually unpaid, but where the workload is particularly heavy they may be paid. The Philadelphia Board holds public hearings one full day each week and one day's private preliminary meeting: members are paid $50 a meeting but not more than $5000 a year. Baltimore pays its Appeals Board members some $7000–8000 a year, which was fixed in the 1920's as equivalent to a high court judge's salary in the hope that men of similar caliber would be appointed to the job.

The work of the Board of Appeals is usually limited to hearing appeals from decisions or interpretations of enforcement officials, and granting "variances" whereby an individual is permitted to exceed the restrictions laid down in the zoning ordinance. The Board's authority derives from the state enabling legislation, which customarily sets specific limits to the Board's discretion. A variance can usually be granted only if there are "practical difficulties or unnecessary hardships" caused by strict enforcement of the ordinance. Traditionally, this was intended to mean physical difficulties peculiar to the site, and financial or personal hardship is of no account unless it is not shared by other owners in the same use zone. Until recently it was often possible to drive a horse and cart through this provision, but over the years the courts have defined more precisely the circumstances in which relief may be granted and the newer ordinances usually spell these out in detail. The most frequent provision makes it clear that the Board may not grant a variance in the *use* of land or buildings but only in the more detailed controls. The provisions in the Chicago ordinance are given on pages 182–183. To set the limits of the Appeals Board's authority as rigidly as Chicago does is probably unwise. The variance procedure in the proposed Boston ordinance would rely largely on a report from the planning department that the requested variance was necessary and reasonably harmless. It certainly seems sensible to avail the Appeals Board of the planning department's technical advice, but this is rarely done.

The Board of Appeals is also required to pass on applications for special exceptions or conditional use permits where these are provided for. The tendency to apply this discretionary procedure to too wide a range of uses has led the lawyers who act as watchdogs in these matters to demand precise standards for the granting of such exceptions and precise limits on the conditions that may be attached to the Board's consent. As in the case of variances, this has recently resulted in some ordinances that tie the Board's hands in a web of specific limitations. It would be far better to repose a little more confidence in the Board of Appeals, bearing in mind that the reasonableness and legality of their actions are subject to review by the courts.

3. *Amendments.* The power to amend zoning regulations or district boundaries resides in the legislative body (the city council). For this reason it is not usual for the ordinance to restrict the scope for amending the text of the regulations. Amendments to the district boundaries, however, are more liable to abuse, and such action has often been made subject to restraints in the state enabling legislation. Frequently it was provided that if the change in zone was opposed by a certain proportion of adjoining owners, or by the planning commission, the amendment required the approval of more than a simple majority of the council—usually two-thirds. This did not prevent innumerable discretionary amendments, however, and the term "spot zoning" became the most heinous in the zoning vocabulary. As a check on this practice the new Chicago ordinance provides that no land shall be rezoned unless it has a frontage of at least

100 feet or an area of 10,000 square feet or is adjacent to a similar use zone. It is a minimal safeguard, and the only remarkable thing is that it should be found to be necessary.

4. *Review.* Broadly speaking, the American citizen may appeal to the courts against any administrative or legislative action on a point of law (constitutional or otherwise), or on grounds that the action was arbitrary, capricious, oppressive, or unreasonable, or represented an abuse of authority. This allows almost any administrative decision or legislative act to be brought before the courts, but the scope for judicial reversal of those actions is more limited.

In zoning matters litigation may take the form either of challenging the constitutionality or legality of the whole ordinance or part of it, or of disputing the reasonableness of the authority's exercise of that power in a particular case.

Thirty-five years have passed since the United States Supreme Court in the Euclid decision declared that "it must be said before the ordinance can be declared unconstitutional, that such provisions are clearly arbitrary and unreasonable, having no substantial relation to the public health, safety, morals, or general welfare"; yet courts are still asked to review the constitutionality of zoning and each year the decisions become more heavily weighted with favorable precedents. Cases have more often been won on the grounds that the methods or drafting of the ordinance exceeded the specific powers granted in the state enabling legislation. Recent innovations in the scope and technique of zoning, however, may reopen the constitutional question of where the uncompensated restriction of property values under the police power becomes an illegal taking of private property.

Judicial review of particular applications of the zoning controls is much more akin to the Minister's jurisdiction in the British system. The U.S. Courts have made it clear that, if the action is within the legal authority of the board or council and is not plainly capricious or discriminatory, they will not substitute their judgment for that of the duly appointed body.

There is a marked tendency in America to regard controversy over land use as a matter for judicial rather than administrative review. But planning is essentially a governmental not a judicial responsibility, or should be if planning is seen as a means of promoting the public interest rather than resolving conflicts of private interest. The effects of the courts' role in the planning process are considered further in Part V.

Subdivision Regulations

Definition and Origin

Subdivision regulations are the controls governing not the use of land or the type of buildings, but the preliminary stages of development: the layout of streets and lots and the provision of necessary services, etc. They occupy a somewhat anomalous position between the building code and the zoning ordinance. Most subdivision regulations apply uniformly to all new residential development, but the model forms suggested by the Federal Housing Agency recommend separate standards according to the character and density of the development. This makes obvious sense but is more akin to zoning controls and has rarely been adopted. Many recent subdivision laws relate required improvements to the availability of public services: if a main line sewer is within reasonable distance new development must link onto it, but if none is available then septic tanks are permitted.

The origin of subdivision regulations is distinct enough. They had to do with the legal requirements for registration of land ownership and transfer, and with the layout of streets. They were essentially "paper" requirements: a proposed road had to be recorded but it did not have to be built nor did roads in one development have to bear any relation to those in another.

Development Standards

The use of this system to enforce rational street layouts and more recently, to require reasonable standards of development, came later than the use of zoning controls. It is usually argued that registration of a subdivision is a "privilege" which the community confers on the developer, in return for which he must comply with the requirements of the regulations, and that therefore these can go far wider than zoning which confers no compensating advantage. It is an artificial distinction and a highly dubious one from the developer's point of view. Both zoning and subdivision regulations are exercised under the police power, and the scope of one should not be wider than the other. But the distinction now seems to be accepted, and the scope of the controls has been steadily extended. They now cover many aspects of development which might better be dealt with in the zoning ordinance, on the analogy of such controls as lot size, frontage, open space, and parking requirements. A survey by the American Society of Planning Officials in 1952 showed the range of requirements in cities of over 10,000 population that had adopted subdivision controls since 1940 (Table II).

Table II

Type of Improvement Required	Number of Cities
Graded streets	85
Minimum surfacing	42
Optimum surfacing	36
Curbs	41
Gutters	30
Sidewalks	53
Storm drainage	55
Sanitary sewers	60
Water supply	55
Street signs	11
Fire hydrants	10
Street trees	25
Gas mains	10
Electricity	8
Street lighting	12

The policy behind such requirements is that all necessary improvements should be provided by the developer rather than at public expense. A survey by the Regional Plan Association, also made in 1952, showed how the responsibility for various improvements was shared between the developer and the municipality in various cities in the New York region (Table III):

Table III Costs of Improvements Borne by Different Agencies*

	A	B	C	None
Grading of streets	98%	0%	2%	0%
Surfacing	96	2	2	0
Curbs	87	0	2	11
Gutters	64	0	2	34
Sidewalks	72	0	6	22
Water mains	83	8	9	0
Sanitary sewers	70	0	2	28
Storm water drains	85	2	0	13
Fire hydrants	46	46	2	6
Streetlights	15	57	6	22
Street signs	28	53	0	19
Street trees	49	25	2	24
Recreation areas	38	21	0	41

A = by developer
B = by municipality
C = by other means
None = no requirement

* Figures are percentages of the cities covered by the survey.

These tables show the wide range of improvements that may be required, and the wide differences among cities in the scope of control. Most of the large cities, which set the pace in zoning practices, have little vacant land and therefore have little interest in subdivision control. Neither Chicago nor New York has adopted such controls and the basic requirements are covered by other laws.

Subdivision control has been studied far less than zoning, and it has also resulted in far less litigation. The Supreme Court has never passed on the validity of such controls, but they have had a relatively easy passage in the lower courts.

The Coordinating Function

There is now a distinct trend toward using subdivision control not only to secure reasonably well constructed development but also to promote certain broader planning objectives. Some planning directors say frankly that they consider subdivision control a more effective device than zoning in securing a satisfactory pattern of new development. One reason for this confidence is certainly that subdivision regulations, unlike zoning controls, are usually administered by the planning department.[3] Not only does this mean that the regulations are interpreted with an awareness of their planning functions, but it also brings the planning staff into direct contact with the developer and affords ample scope for negotiation and advice. The newer regulations are often fairly brief but provide specifically for the details of the proposal to be worked out between the developer and the authority. Some cities also use the subdivision procedure to secure coordination among city departments (streets, fire, police, health, parks) that have an interest in the servicing of new residential areas. To advise the planning commission on new subdivision, El Paso has established a committee that consists of representatives of all city departments, the school districts, public utilities such as water, and even private utilities such as electric power and telephone companies and the Southern Pacific Railroad. It seems to be working remarkably well. It both facilitates thorough review of proposals and relieves the developer of much negotiation with separate agencies.

Neighborhood Development

The improved procedures and broadened scope of subdivision control are chiefly aimed at securing better neighborhood planning. It is one thing to ensure that the developer does a responsible job in constructing adequate roads and

3. The fact that they are administered by the appointed planning commission rather than the elected city council has become a point of adverse criticism: but there remains the safeguard of judicial review.

services; it is another to secure a full range of community facilities—schools, parks, etc.—well planned in relation to new development; and still another to achieve compact development well coordinated with existing uses and ensuring convenience for the residents and economic provision of public services.

The problem of securing adequate land for public uses in new residential areas is often dealt with in either of two rather extraordinary ways. Many cities have required developers to donate part of their land for public use. Other cities require a financial contribution to the cost of providing parks, etc., on the basis of so much per lot. This is often done where the size of individual developments is too small to provide adequate areas for public use. The propriety of such requirements seems highly dubious, and the more usual procedure in new ordinances is to permit the planning department to designate on the developer's application those areas which will be required for public use; the city must then acquire them at fair market value within a stated period (usually one year), failing which they revert to the developer. Even so, it is customary to provide for the "voluntary" dedication of land for public use, and the planning department does what it can to cajole the developer into being public-spirited. It is a typically American way of doing business, and developers are aware that provision of schools, parks, and so forth, is a major selling point with prospective homebuyers.

The most comprehensive proposals for "planning by subdivision control" are the draft regulations for Phoenix, Arizona, which is the most rapidly growing city in America. Besides covering all the normal layout and construction standards, the proposed ordinance would also require the developer to submit a "Development Master Plan" showing the proposed land uses, road pattern, sites for schools, parks, and so forth. The ordinance then defines the criteria by which the planning department shall pass judgment on these proposals (see pages 184–187). Most of the conditions that the proposed development must meet are defined in the zoning and subdivision ordinances, but there remains a fairly wide area of discretion as regards the layout of large-scale developments and the subdivision controls themselves usually afford considerable flexibility.

Subdivision regulations may also deal with other aspects of development—for example, preservation of fine trees or prohibition of what is delightfully called "promiscuous bulldozing"—i.e., the appalling practice of leveling every site to a dull flatness or shearing away hilltops. The area in which subdivision controls may become of prime importance, however, is in the "programming" of new development.

Programming

One of the characteristic features of suburban development in America is its lack of contiguity. Individual developers use whatever land they can acquire quickly and cheaply; universal car ownership overcomes the deterrent of isolation; vacant sites left behind by the outward spread of suburbia seldom get filled in later; the result is a patchwork of development, unsightly, wasteful, inconvenient, and expensive to service.

Perhaps the worst deficiency of American land-use controls has been their failure to prevent this process. The traditional zoning ordinance allocates all land in the city to some type of private development (courts ruled that this was necessary to afford equal protection of the law); it deals with the "what" but not with the "when." Subdivision regulations, although they were intended chiefly to prevent a chaotic road pattern, were never adequate to prevent piecemeal development. And this is not surprising since, in the absence of a system of financial compensation for denying development values, the initiative for deciding the rate and location of development must remain with the developer. Despite the encouragement that a few court decisions have given to exclusionist policies in some small communities (by supporting high minimum standards designed to prevent lower-class housing) the only defensible policy is to ensure that while sufficient land is available to meet the market demand for development of all types, such development is adapted to an orderly process of community growth.

The controlling factor must be the economical and adequate provision of public services. This was certainly one of the chief benefits that the originators of zoning saw in the system, and although it was obscured by the importance attached to "nuisance" analogies and maintenance of private property values, it remains the most cogent argument for development control. A detailed plan for the extension of public services (water, sewerage, schools, parks) that has been related to the anticipated demand from new development provides the surest basis for the effective control of suburban growth. The relationship should be that private development determines the *pace* (tempo) of public development, but that public development determines the *place* (sequence) of private development. Once this relationship has been established by factual analysis of projected growth and planned extension of services, the location of new development can be controlled on a reasonable basis.

There is growing awareness of this need in America, but the methods of control so far devised are somewhat clumsy and indirect. The most common method is to zone the outer fringes of the undeveloped area for very low density residential development (a minimum lot size of one to five acres is not infrequent and has been upheld by the courts). But this wastes land and can encourage development that will later impede growth of the city; in some cases the developer simply doubles the depth of the lot and the houseowner has a property sixty feet wide and a thousand feet long. Where land is plentiful, it is frontage, not depth, that costs money. A more promising method is the "agricultural zone" described earlier in this chapter, but this device generally would not apply to vacant land not in agricultural use or of low fertility, and it is the abundance of this land that presents the problem.

Finding that zoning is inadequate for the purpose, planners are turning to the only other tool generally available—subdivision regulation. Two methods are being tried. One is to set such exacting standards of development—broad pavements, granite curbs, street lighting, etc.—that it is profitable to build only in areas zoned for high-density use. The zoning districts can then be adjusted to facilitate orderly expansion. But this method impedes low-density residential development for which there is usually a strong demand and which may well be desirable. The second method, now being used in a few cities, is to require that new development take place only where there is an adequate range of community facilities and public services. This is frequently based on the authority of the public health department, which is often more influential than the planning department. Several cities require that all new residences be linked to the public sewer system or water supply. New development can then be programmed in relation to an orderly extension of these services, and in other areas only a very limited range of development is allowed, sometimes on a temporary basis. Such a system presupposes a really competent survey and planning process to decide the areas of high and low priority, backed up by a consistent program of public works.[4] Where a community has decided to exert con-

4. The two cases which seem to have discouraged this type of program planning are not by any means definitive. In *Reid Development Corporation v. Parsippany—Troy Hills Township* (New Jersey 1952), the court held that extension of water facilities was the developer's right and could not be withheld as a means of coercing him to meet certain requirements in the subdivision controls. They said, however, that "such benefits are to be had through the channels prescribed by law . . . planning and zoning powers may not be exercised by indirection." This appears to mean that denial of water supply is an improper means of enforcement (presumably the controls must be explicit and enforceable by injunction or criminal prosecution). But it does not suggest that the controls may not be designed so as to further economy in the planned provision of services. In *Beach v. Planning and Zoning Commission of Town of Milford* (Connecticut 1954) the court declined to uphold the Commission's action in refusing to approve a plat, which met all the subdivision law requirements, on the grounds that the needs of the proposed development for public services (schools, police protection) would place a financial burden on the town which it was not able to meet. The court based its decision on the fact that the enabling legislation did not allow this as a ground for refusal, but in any event there is every difference between refusing to allow any new development, and in-

trol over its future growth, and has succeeded in coordinating all the agencies of public development, the latter method seems very promising and well within reasonable exercise of the police power. The other methods, which depend on artificially high or wasteful minimum standards, are crude and essentially irrelevant. Despite the beginnings of a rational system of programming in a few cities, this undoubtedly remains the worst flaw in the American control of private development.

Open Space

Traditionally, the preservation of open country for its recreational or landscape value has been the function of the federal and state rather than local governments, and the policy has always been to acquire the areas outright rather than to protect them by other methods.[5] This is, of course, because the normal land-use controls carry no compensation. In some ways this has been an advantage. With the land in public ownership, there are no problems about access or protection of legitimate private interests, and the areas can be fully developed and utilized for public enjoyment.

Despite the rampant pace of development, a remarkable amount of America has been preserved in this way. Nearly twenty percent of California is preserved as state or national parks and forests; only twenty-eight miles of Oregon's 400-mile Pacific coastline remains in private ownership. The twenty-nine National Parks in nineteen states cover 13 million acres, and they are magnificent. Not only do they include some of the most superb and unspoiled scenery in the

---

sisting that new development conform to the planned provision of public services. Overloading an inadequate system of public services is no argument against development (except as a temporary expedient while services are extended), but distorting a planned system which provides adequately for orderly growth seems a very sound argument for control.

5. For a full account of present and future policies, see the reports of President Johnson's Task Force on the Preservation of Natural Beauty. Cf. also the Land and Water Conservation Fund Act 1965, and the Highway Beautification Act 1965.

world, but they have been made truly accessible both by
excellent mountain roads and thousands of miles of horse
and foot trails, and by very good "interpretive services"—
entertaining and well-designed miniature museums covering
the ecology and geology of the area, its Indian prehistory,
and its place in the story of westward discovery and settlement, and talks and guided hikes by the admirable park
rangers. Glacier, Olympic, and Yellowstone are all over a
thousand square miles in area. There are also eighty-three
National Monuments, mostly of archaeological interest,
smaller in area than the National Parks but often quite extensive. In addition, there are 149 National Forests covering
180 million acres, and recreational use of these is encouraged. They include seventy "wildernesses"—areas which,
unlike the National Parks, are completely undeveloped and
accessible only on foot or horseback. These are some of the
largest and most exciting reservations in America. Selway-
Bitterroot is over 2,800 square miles, and another area of
1,900 square miles adjoins it across the Salmon River in
Idaho. There are also 290 National Wildlife Refuges, including the 3159-square-mile Desert Game Range in southern Nevada. And besides the federal lands there are
hundreds of state parks, some of them very extensive.

Outright purchase is certainly the most satisfactory
method where the land is to be developed primarily for
recreational use or as a reservation, but there remains the
problem of agriculture and other open land that should remain in private ownership but needs to be protected from
incongruous development. It is here that the hiatus in the
American system between uncompensated control and public acquisition is most apparent. In an effort to overcome
this, the idea of "conservation easements" has recently been
introduced. The suggestion is that the public should acquire
not the freehold but only the conservation or development
"easement" of land that it wants to see kept permanently as
open space. The easement could be acquired by gift or by
voluntary or compulsory purchase. This method has already
been used for a good many years to acquire "scenic easements" along major highways; the National Park Service

acquired 177 such easements covering 1,468 acres along the Blue Ridge Parkway (a splendid road running 400 miles along the Appalachians from the Shenandoah National Park near Washington, D. C., to the Great Smokies in Tennessee). It seems a quite promising idea, and is the subject of a very interesting report by W. H. Whyte "Securing Open Space for Urban America," published by the Urban Land Institute in October 1959.

Whether the idea will be widely adopted is very uncertain. Besides the problem of securing legislation, there are some disadvantages in the system itself. The public would not have access to the land. The American farmer apparently does not share the English landowner's sense of noblesse oblige, and field footpaths are almost unknown. It may prove very difficult to devise a uniform type of deed, and the scheme may get bogged down in legal difficulties. Even where an easement is acquired, it is not likely to secure the land permanently against the pressure for development. The method is clearly open to misuse, and if it is to be used fairly then it will have to be used extensively if some landowners are not to profit at the expense of others. The legal and political strategy, and the orders of priority, will be very ticklish problems. As a footnote to his study, Whyte quotes the councillors of San Jose, California, who were so outraged by his favorable comment in *Life* magazine on Santa Clara County's agricultural zoning that they adopted an official protest to Time, Inc. The city manager wrote that "The greenbelt, in our booming society, is an anachronism."

A more satisfactory way of preserving open country while retaining it in agricultural or other private use would be for the public to acquire the land and lease it back for private occupancy. But to most Americans this smacks of "socialism," or worse. Fortunately, America is so vast a country that while the few major metropolitan areas may continue their debauched development, there will remain millions of acres open and unspoiled. The best hope probably lies in using the accepted controls on urban development to secure more compact and orderly growth, rather than in establishing more or less tenuous legal safeguards for undeveloped land. Land needed for the enjoyment of teeming metropolis had better be bought outright.

Taxation and Other Fiscal Measures

Most types of land-use control, in America as in Britain, are often stigmatized as "negative." Controls which prevent bad development are not particularly negative in their effect, but there is always a demand for more "positive" measures to encourage good or necessary development. Obviously one can stimulate almost any activity by offering a large enough financial inducement; the question is how great an incentive is required to induce the appropriate response. There is a good deal of interest in such measures in America, but very few, if any, are notably successful and some (such as the immense system of federal insurance for private mortgages and other financial transactions) seem largely superfluous. Public measures to compensate for the inadequacies of the free market and private institutions may well discourage attempts to remedy those inadequacies.

Examples of inducements offered to private enterprise to promote necessary types of development are the following:

1. Exemption from real-estate taxes for limited periods for certain types of low-income housing and for limited rental housing, or for new industrial development; (of doubtful legality but widely used to attract new investment).
2. Exemption from corporate taxation (e.g., housing cooperatives).
3. Income tax concessions in the form of accelerated depreciation allowances (e.g., defense plant financing).
4. Mortgage insurance (Federal Housing Administration).
5. Federal insurance of deposits in Savings and Loans Association (a main source of financing house purchase).

All such interventions by public authorities in private enterprise development may be accompanied by some degree of public control over the undertaking, and, inevitably, public funds require adequate auditing. In America, the success of the incentives tends to decrease in relation to the extent of control.

Much the most striking of these "positive" measures is, of course, the urban renewal program, in which the local authority uses its power of compulsory acquisition to assemble sites large enough for comprehensive redevelopment and sells them to private developers. The difference between the cost of making the land available and the price it will fetch in the open market is borne two-thirds by the federal government and one-third by the local authority.

Urban Renewal

The aspect of the urban renewal program most relevant to this report is the type of land-use controls which can be employed where there exists a contractual relationship between a public authority and a private developer.

Different redevelopment agencies have widely varying approaches to this problem. Some, as in Chicago, regard their main job as that of assembling and clearing the land, and selling it as soon as possible to the highest bidder, leaving the private developer to decide how to develop the site subject only to a basic land-use plan and the normal zoning controls. The Chicago agency gets all its land-use controls onto one page of the redevelopment contract. Other agencies, as in Washington and New Haven (where nearly a tenth of the city has been cleared for redevelopment) believe that the opportunity should be seized to exert the maximum possible control over the quality of the new development. In these cases the redevelopment plan spells out in very considerable detail the controls necessary to bring about the desired type of development (an example from the New Haven Church Street project is given on pages 188–191).

The agencies that believe in exercising detailed control are finding that conventional "minimum standard" controls are not sufficient to secure really good results. Consequently, more attention is now being given to stating the objectives of redevelopment more precisely, so that these criteria, rather than the detailed controls, will guide the developers in making their proposals and the agency in assessing them. These statements of objectives tend to be of three kinds: first, the broad objectives of redevelopment; second, a more precise statement of the type of development envisaged; and third, the criteria, in addition to the foregoing, by which the competing proposals will be judged.

An example of the first type are the objectives set for the Southwest Urban Renewal Area in Washington, D. C., one of the largest renewal sites in the country. Here are a few of the stated objectives:

(a) To reestablish Southwest Washington as a major physical and economic asset to the City of Washington, appropriate to the National Capital;

(b) To continue in the Project Area residential neighborhoods near the central business district and within walking distance of nearby government offices and establishments;

(c) To provide suitable locations and good environment for a cross section of housing types and accommodations, including those for the lower-middle income group, needed and marketable in the District and to provide opportunities for owner occupancy of individual residential units as well as to provide a substantial proportion of residential units suitable for rent or sale to middle-income families;

(h) To provide a new and more agreeable entrance to the Southwest along Tenth Street, and to give the waterfront area a more direct connection with the Mall, government buildings, and the central business district;

(k) To provide a modern town center as a focus for the surrounding residential neighborhoods with essential commercial and community facilities including off-street parking, parks, and sites for churches;

(m) To develop the waterfront within the Project Area along the approved bulkhead line for service to the marinas, for community recreational facilities, and for access and service to pier structures;

(n) To provide areas for limited second commercial uses appropriate to the strategic location of the Project Area;

(o) To preserve significant historic structures whenever possible; and

(p) To provide maximum opportunity for development by private enterprise.

The second type of statement includes a detailed description of the purposes for which the cleared land shall be used, and this may be very specific: San Francisco wants a Japanese Cultural Center and housing for "senior citizens" in its Western Extension project; Washington wants a hotel of not more than two hundred rooms in its Columbia Plaza scheme. New Haven states that the commercial part of its Church Street project must accord with the following criteria:

(a) The proposed uses shall be distributed over the area of the four blocks in a manner to create optimum reuse and shall not be concentrated within a portion of the total area.
(b) The various frontages will be developed with continuous related uses in order to produce the greatest impact as an integrated unit.
(c) The proposed uses shall be developed to create a center which will be commercially attractive and a focal point of social interest for the community as a whole.
(d) The various elements of the plan shall be connected by an internal pedestrian circulation system designed as an integral part of the development, so as to create for the pedestrian comfort and ease of movement within the proposed structures.
(e) The services (i.e. parking and trucking) to the proposed uses must be integrated with pedestrian and vehicular circulation patterns, as may be the case, both inside and outside the development area.
(f) The concept and design must reflect the most advanced architectural concepts and technique so as to provide lasting interest and strength.

These, of course, are chiefly matters of design, and several cities, having been disappointed at the failure of the early schemes to produce anything worth looking at, are now trying to define what they mean by good design, or rather, what qualities a good design should have. An example is the "Design Objectives" set by the Washington agency for its Columbia Plaza project (see pages 192–193).

Third, especially where there is strong competition for the development contract, the agency has to be careful to state the criteria by which it will judge the proposals. For example, the San Francisco agency in calling for bids on its Golden Gateway project (a superb site) announced that after a review of the proposals and a public hearing, the agency would make its choice "on the basis of the following considerations":

1. Quality and amenities offered in design of apartment units.
2. Balance in range of size of apartments.
3. Balance in range of estimated rental charges (or costs to owners if cooperative or community apartments are planned).
4. Architectural excellence and its contribution to the appearance of the entire neighborhood, including relationship to landscape, marine and park views, pedestrian ways, and to the avoidance of monotony.
5. Highest prices offered for land.
6. Experience and financial responsibility of developer or developer group.

In the event, the agency received proposals from most of the country's outstanding developers and some groups specially formed for the purpose, all employing first-rate architects and all bidding high. It was reported that the cost of the design work, presentation and models totaled over $1 million. Faced with this avalanche of talent the agency (a board of laymen with only a very small architectural staff) decided to ask a group of America's topnotch architects and planners to act as their advisors. The chairman of this panel, Mario Ciampi, drew up a list of twenty-nine "basic questions" to guide the group in assessing the proposals (see pages 194–196). Their report has not yet been published, but it is said that, not surprisingly, the panel found some things to admire in each proposal but none which seemed conclusively the best.

The problem of seeking quality in redevelopment is generally agreed to be the most exacting faced by renewal agencies. There is a widespread feeling that the program will have failed unless it helps to create an urban environment which is humane, stimulating, varied, and enjoyable: qualities for which none of the completed schemes is conspicuous. New Haven has decided that the only way to tackle the problem is for the renewal agency (or the planning department) to undertake a detailed design of the project area—not merely a land-use plan but a complete architectural treatment. It is not intended that this should be forced on the developer, who is to be left free to produce his own ideas; but only in this way, it is felt, can the agency be sure of what it wants to achieve, and only by such detailed study can controls be designed to secure the right result. An alternative approach urged by some experienced officials is to abandon any attempt to control or assess the quality of the design (which includes much more than aesthetic considerations) and to judge the proposals purely on economic criteria: the bid, the contribution to the city's tax base, the provision of suitable housing and employment, etc.

No doubt an adequate assessment of redevelopment proposals should include both aspects. If adequate measures of land-use control with respect to urban renewal projects can be evolved, they may well find their way into the system of land-use control governing purely private development.

Private Controls

In conclusion, it is entertaining to look at the controls that private developers impose on themselves and their customers. If the controls exercised by public authorities over land-use in America seem excessively detailed and capricious, the controls happily adopted by private citizens are positively sadistic. Many of America's most exclusive residential neighborhoods are governed by a formidable armory of restrictive covenants that cover everything from painting the front door to hanging out the washing (not allowed). Such covenants are as old as property law, of course, but they have become remarkably prolific.

The first American developer to use restrictive covenants to govern the character of a whole neighborhood was the

Roland Park Company of Baltimore some eighty years ago. The development still exists and includes America's first planned shopping center (1887). It was followed in the next decade by several more planned developments in the "garden district" of Baltimore. Among the controls adopted was a requirement that all properties must be resold through the agency of the development company. In addition, the householder accepts almost every other restrictive covenant known to man. The company undertook all maintenance work—snow clearing, removing leaves, etc.—for a fixed annual fee which by an embarrassing legal flaw remains now what it was in 1900. The company loses $30,000 a year on maintenance costs but recovers it through commissions on sales. The development is undoubtedly one of the best maintained and most attractive residential suburbs in America, and probably in any other country. There are many similar examples, among them Palos Verdes Estates in California, the Country Club District in Kansas, the Home Ranch Park near Santa Barbara, California, and all the better parts of Houston, Texas, which has no public control of land use at all.

It is a measure of the success of these private controls that they have been taken up in a big way by America's largest developers—Levitt and Sons, the builders of Levittowns. The Levitt organization has built suburban towns of around 17,000 homes (50,000–60,000 population) in New York (Long Island), Pennsylvania, and New Jersey. The towns have often been criticized as the epitome of suburbia, but in the latest development not only do the Levitts sell houses at 40 percent below the normal market price, with a truckload of kitchen and laundry appliances and some twenty small trees and bushes in the garden; but they also donate all church sites, and build, equip, and donate all the necessary schools together with such neighborhood facilities as an Olympic-size swimming pool for every thousand families. With a little more intelligent planning and some more usable open space (and perhaps some industry, though they are located near major employment centers), they would not fall so very far short of Britain's modified version of Ebenezer Howard's garden city.

But along with the dishwasher and shrubbery comes a huge list of restrictive covenants, which Levitt and Sons summarize as follows in their handy "Homeowners' Guide—some information for residents of Levittown to help them enjoy their new homes":

Every fine residential community must have restrictions on property uses to insure the maintenance of its high standards. As a result, property values increase and greater enjoyment accrues to all homeowners. Here is a summary of the restrictions at Levittown. If you read them carefully, you will see that they have but one purpose: to protect you and your neighbors from practices that would be detrimental to your property. For that reason the restrictions will be strictly enforced.

1. (a) You may add an ATTACHED room or garage to your house. It must be similar in architecture, color and material to the original dwelling, and the addition must not project in front of the dwelling at all.
(b) On an interior lot, a rear addition may project up to 15 feet, provided that there is then left at least 20 feet of open rear yard. A side addition must leave at least 6 feet of open yard on each side, and a total of 13 feet on both sides.
(c) On a corner lot, each side of the house facing a street is considered a front. If your house fronts on two streets, a side or rear addition must leave at least 6 feet on one interior side and 20 feet on the other. If you bought one of the corner properties fronting on three streets, you must leave at least 6 feet on the interior side.
(d) Before you actually make any addition to your home, be sure to check the zoning ordinance and building code of the township. These, as well as the above property restrictions, must be complied with; and it may also be necessary for you to obtain a building permit from the township.

2. You may display a residence sign but it can't be more than one square foot in size. If you light it, don't use colored, flashing, unshielded or spot lighting. This could be very annoying to your neighbors.
3. You may keep not more than two domesticated household

pets (dogs, cats, etc.) but no commercial breeding or harboring is allowed.

4. If you are a physician, dentist, chiropractor, chiropodist, optometrist, attorney, accountant or engineer, you may have your office in your home. But NO BUSINESS OF ANY KIND IS PERMITTED—the residential sections of Levittown must remain residential. No more than one family may occupy a house. Incidentally, no trucks or other commercial vehicles may be garaged on the property except for the temporary servicing of the premises.

5. When you put your garbage out for collection make sure it is in a tightly closed metal container. Don't strew rubbish or garbage around your property.

6. You may plant a shrub or other growing fence BUT don't let it grow higher than 3 feet. NO FABRICATED FENCES (WOOD, METAL, ETC.) WILL BE PERMITTED. In designing the blocks and lots at Levittown we have achieved the maximum open and spacious appearance. Fences will cut this up into small parcels and spoil the whole effect no matter how good-looking the fence material itself may be—and some of it is or can become pretty terrible! This item is of prime importance.

7. Laundry must be hung *only* in the rear yard on a revolving portable type dryer which must be taken down when not actually in use. Old-fashioned clothes lines strung across the lawn or house look messy and are prohibited. And please don't leave laundry hanging out on Sundays and holidays when you and your neighbors are most likely to be relaxing on your rear lawn.

8. If you property backs on a road, the lot has been made at least 20 feet deeper than usual. This is so the rear 20 feet can be landscaped and screened, thereby protecting your privacy from passing automobiles and pedestrians. You must—and we're sure you'll want to—take care of this landscaping. With reasonable attention it will soon grow thick and high enough to give you complete privacy. This is the one and only place where shrub fencing is permitted to grow higher than 3 feet (see item 6 above).

9. Lawns must be mowed and weeds removed at least once a week between April 15th and November 15th. Nothing makes a lawn—and a neighborhood—look shabbier than uncut grass and unsightly weeds. A lot of thought, work and money has gone into the preparation of your lawn. It will flourish if you take care of it—but will quickly grow wild and unkempt if you don't.

10. If you live on a corner you cannot remove or add anything to the planting at the corner. Should anything die, you must replant the same items, if we don't. We go to special pains on corners and that's why we don't want them changed.

11. You or any other property owner in your section (as well as this Company) have the right to take legal steps to enforce these restrictions and eliminate violations by others.

12. The exterior material and color of each house have been carefully selected for pleasing and harmonious variety in the neighborhood. They must not be changed.

The public control of private development could never go so far—in America or anywhere else.

V UTILITY

Most American critics of land-use control begin with the observation that control is all right in theory but a political football in operation. The susceptibility of land-use control to political and other pressures is chiefly responsible for the American insistence on reducing as much of the control as possible to standardized requirements. It has also led to the Penelope-like pursuit of setting standards for permitted exceptions to the general standards.

Assuming, however, that the system is honestly administered, is it effective? There are three aspects worth considering: the benefits of the system in securing decent standards of development; its utility as a means of implementing a development plan; and its success, as a formalized system with judicial review, in lightening the administrative burden of control and securing consistency.

Development Standards

America shares with Britain a striking capacity for making a mess of her environment. But America carries it to extremes. The northeastern seaboard from Boston to Baltimore is a twentieth-century slum of unparalleled squalor. It is tolerable only where a turnpike cuts anonymously through the countryside, or a loop of parkway skirts the unending dreariness of U.S. Route 1 with a mile-wide artificial landscape. But further west, man-made ugliness is swallowed up by the immense distances and the grandeur of the country. After driving a hundred miles or so through the Arizona desert one is relieved rather than horrified to see the jaunty billboards sprouting between the saguaros as the next road town approaches. The rough wooden buildings, the thick utility lines strung along the roadside, the scattered houses —all have the look of a frontier town which it would be ridiculous to criticize because it looks untidy. Against the vast background of America, the critical standards of Subtopia are irrelevant.

90

But in the chaos of a highly competitive urban society, and in the burgeoning suburbs, the public control of private development becomes a really urgent concern. To assess the benefits of normal zoning and subdivision controls, one has only to explore a city that has none. There are plenty of these in America. Many communities have not even adopted building or safety codes, let alone the more fanciful controls on land use. In 1951 the New York State Building Code Commission found that of the 1,500 municipalities in the state, only 339 had adopted a building code.

The classic example of the city with no land-use controls is Houston, Texas, the only city of anything like its size (around 900,000) with that distinction. Unfortunately for the planning advocate, the first, and indeed the dominant, impression of the city is that of a typical south central metropolis, not at all dissimilar from rival Dallas (which has the whole planning apparatus), with a rather striking amount of parkland near the city center, and with some fine residential neighborhoods. The main reason for the high residential standards, however, is that in the absence of public control, private developers surround their projects with a barrier of restrictive covenants, generally much tighter than zoning would be.

The effects of no control are to be seen in the less well-to-do areas of the city, where the lack of density controls produces really bad conditions. Apartments are built to absurd densities on grossly inadequate sites. Most cheaper houses, notably in the Negro quarters, are badly over-crowded, with no setback from the pavement and prac-tically no space between buildings. Oddly enough this was also evident in one of the most expensive new developments —Walnut Bend. Here was a site eight miles from the city center with homes in the $30,000 class, yet side yards were so inadequate that in one case the fancy roofs of two neigh-boring houses overlapped. But the worst effects are naturally in the cheapest developments. In the absence of subdivision requirements, about 80 percent of new residential develop-ments provide normal site improvements (surfaced roads, sidewalks, sewers, and drainage) because the market demands them; but that leaves 20 percent ready-made slums.

Most people I talked with in Houston—bankers, real estate men, and planners (there is a planning department with a large budget, engaged chiefly in public works planning)—agreed that on the whole the large-scale developer, the builder of higher-income homes, and the better-educated home buyer were all aware of the need to protect their investments, and that private covenants were adequate for the purpose. The big investor and the intelligent citizen are able to protect their interests, but the "small man" can and does suffer. For example, where a development of small homes in a poorer neighborhood adjoins vacant land, there is every likelihood that this land will be developed for some incompatible or blighting commercial use. This immediately affects the value of the homes and very probably the owners will be unable to sell because banks will not renew the loans. There are other commercial lending institutions that lend on substandard or depreciated property, but at a much higher rate that may halve the sale price.

Industry is not a serious problem: its own location requirements guide it to large undeveloped areas along major transport routes, and high land costs force it outside the city. As always, the really intractable use is the low-status commercial—the shoestring operations that clutter up every American city. There certainly seem to be more of these in Houston than anywhere else, stretching out along every approach to the city in an endless string of barbecue stands, drive-in laundries, bars, used-car lots, tenth grade shopping centers—"you name it." The home builder always leaves the main road frontage of his development unbuilt on, since its speculative value leaps up when the houses are occupied. As a result, nearly every residential sector has a thick fringe of unsightly, often impoverished, commercial development.

In theory, almost everyone (except the land speculator) stands to benefit from the introduction of zoning and subdivision control. But despite successive attempts to get it started in 1926, 1938, 1948, and one now under way, there is little enthusiasm for it. There is a very widespread feeling that zoning maladministered would be worse than no zoning at all. And the lack of any confidence in the political machinery leaves Houston on the horns of an all-American dilemma.

Where reasonable controls have been adopted and are well administered, they do undoubtedly result not only in a sound standard of development and an absence of conflicting uses but also in stability of neighborhood character and maintenance of property values. The average American suburb, once it matures a little, is not a bad place to live, despite the jeremiads of sociologists, and the better residential districts in American cities have a spaciousness, consistency, and charm which is very attractive and unlike anything in Britain.

The extent to which zoning preserves or enhances the value of private property, on which grounds the early legal battles were won, can hardly be calculated. In strictly financial terms, the development values inherent in land must be redistributed by zoning in a less uniform manner than if the market were the sole determinant. Use districting must concentrate high values in certain areas more than a free market in property would and must withhold development potential from the more restricted districts. But the majority of a community is always more concerned with protecting the investment value of property than promoting its speculative value. And this was, and is, the basis for much popular support of zoning. Property owners support it because it tends to promote conformity and stability by restricting the scope for change or competition. Developers support it because stability of use makes development less hazardous and protects investment without the cost of ownership in adjoining property. We (in Britain) may not be accustomed to think of these as planning objectives, but they are reasonable interests for a community to support.

The scope, and to some extent the utility of American land-use controls, will have become apparent from Parts III and IV of this report. On the whole, despite some gerrymandering, some incompetence and some indifference, the controls are effective as far as they go. And the more recent versions go a long way toward controlling all those factors of private development which affect the public interest.

The defects of the American system, on the other hand, might be summarized as follows:

1. The districting device has probably had a deleterious effect in two areas. First, by withholding even the protective benefits of zoning from areas that were already deteriorated or infected by indiscriminate development, it has accelerated blight and impeded rehabilitation. Second, it has placed the emphasis on distinctions between uses rather than on the relationships that tie them together. As a result it has probably acted as a brake on any trend toward a more cohesive environment and has encouraged the fragmentation of urban and suburban life.

2. The standards set were reflections of existing development, and progress in design and technology inevitably rendered them obsolete. Moreover, the standards appropriate to individual private development are often irreconcilable with the needs of modern large-scale projects both public and private.

3. The absence of authority to compensate for injured interests has restricted the ability to influence the character or location of development on open land where existing property interests provide no support or guidance for the exercise of control. In these circumstances certain types of development, notably small-scale, unstable commercial uses, have proved especially difficult to control.

4. It has never been used effectively to control the programming of private development, except where the object has been to discourage housing for low-income families; and the fact that it can be adapted to those ends has brought it no credit.

5. Even the new ordinances, which take account of the relationships between uses, do not take account of relations with other communities.

Most of these deficiencies represent a failure to respond to changing conditions. Since the whole object of American land-use controls is to regulate, not restrict, the process of growth, this deficiency is particularly damaging. Most current thinking is directed to ensuring that the system of control remains well adjusted to the natural process of change and growth. I believe there are signs that it may yet be successful.

Plan Implementation

But sound development standards do not make a well-planned city. In the long term, land-use controls are only as good as the plan which they implement. The most obvious defect in the whole American land-use planning machinery is that the controls came before the planning. It is still very much the exception, rather than the rule, for a city to have an up-to-date development plan. Several cities that are revising their zoning and subdivision regulations have no comprehensive development plan to guide them. This may seem absurd, but many short-staffed planning departments must choose between spending several years on a plan that cannot be legally enforced and setting up a control system to cope with the flood of development that will come, plan or no plan. Much of the survey and analysis on which a development plan must be based, is also necessary to set up a sound zoning system. But the zoning system deals only with private development, and to be an effective planning tool it must be related to a comprehensive plan for public and private development. It is difficult to assess the effectiveness of the American control system in implementing a development plan, when it has rarely been used in such a manner.

A more serious defect in the American system is not in technique but in the lack of power to pay compensation for loss of development value. Without this it is impossible to secure some of the most important objectives of land-use planning. While the American system can be quite effective in resolving conflicts of private interest and in enforcing good standards of private development, its scope for resolving conflicts of public and private interest in land-use is far more limited: it cannot reserve land needed for public use or protect land of high agricultural or amenity value from development. The only way to overcome the first deficiency is to buy land zoned for public use in the development plan as soon as a private development threatens, which may be long before the public need for it arises. There remains the problem of land which is not needed for public use but which should be protected from urban development. Again, the only answer is compensation, by special legislation or by acquiring the land outright and leasing it back to the owner, or by acquiring the conservation easements (see Part IV).

Leaving aside these peculiarities of the American situation—lack of experience and lack of adequate powers—it is still necessary to ask whether a formalized system of controls can ever be as effective as an ad hoc discretionary power of control in implementing a development plan. The answer obviously depends, first, on how effective the ad hoc control actually is, and, second, on how much discretionary power public opinion will tolerate. Apart from these imponderables, does a formalized system make sense?

One reason why so many American planners feel dissatisfied with zoning controls, and why most British observers see no merit in them at all, is that traditional use zoning creates an artificial legal conformity which grossly oversimplifies the facts of life, and to which exceptions have constantly to be made. A British town map may not spell out the pattern of land use in any more detail than an American zoning map (in fact it is less detailed), but it will not be speaking in terms of rigidly exclusive zones; each development proposal can be considered on its merits and in relation to the general intent of the development plan. The more recent innovations in American zoning technique, described in Part IV, are aimed at both refining the categories of use zone and allowing much greater flexibility by introducing in addition to permitted uses, a long list of conditional uses that require a special permit. I do not know whether it is possible to refine such a system of use zoning to the point where it will meet all reasonable requirements. But even if this is not possible, exceptional needs can be met by allowing a modicum of discretion to the planning authority.

A distinction needs to be drawn between a rigid, over-simplified classification of land uses and the codification of subsidiary regulations. It may be that use zoning runs counter to the natural complexity and cohesiveness of urban life, but there seems no reason why, when government decides to apply conditions to different types of land use, those conditions should not be as specific and consistent as possible. For this purpose land uses can be broken down into more detailed categories than the land-use zones permit, and the controls can be adapted fairly precisely to the type of activity or development involved. Again, a little discretionary power will provide the oil to make the system run smoothly. If the controls are sufficiently precise and relevant, important planning objectives can be realized by this means: varied residential densities, well-balanced building height and layout, adequate parking and loading facilities, protection of valuable environmental qualities, preservation of neighborhood identity and character, improved distribution of commercial uses, and improved operational standards in industry. These go a long way toward achieving a convenient and economic arrangement of land use.

Administration and Review

The great question is whether a system with this degree of particularity will become impossibly burdensome to administer. As explained in Part IV, a city planning department is responsible for the administration only of subdivision control, and in that there is considerable scope for negotiation and the tactful exercise of discretionary control. But subdivision control concerns only the layout and preliminary development of land. The basic controls governing land use and all the more detailed development controls are in the zoning ordinance, which is administered by the building inspector's department. In their day-to-day administration, the controls are simply treated as one more specific requirement with which a developer's proposal must comply before a building permit is issued. There is no desire, and very little authority, to interpret the controls in a flexible manner or to depart in any particular from the book of rules. The system simply requires a literal application of specific regulations; it may mean a heavy load of routine work, but there is no inherent difficulty. It must be a much simpler task than that of judging each application for planning permission on its merits and attempting to devise suitable conditions to attach to the consent, or producing adequate reasons for refusal.

Under the American system responsibility for permitting reasonable and necessary departures from the letter of the law rests with the Board of Appeals. The dislike of discretionary control is so great, however, that most Boards of Appeals are happier if their authority also rests on specific conditions. In his annual report for 1955, the chairman of the Philadelphia Board of Zoning Adjustment, urging the need for a revised ordinance, expressed the American philosophy of land-use control very properly:

Zoning cannot be made easy, but if all citizens' rights were more clearly defined in the basic law there would not be so much contentious litigation among neighbors and the Board of Zoning Adjustment would be enabled to make equitable decisions in all cases by use of identical standards.

British planners would probably complain that land-use control does not lend itself to such convenient standardization. But it must be an objective of all control procedures to operate in a consistent manner and in accordance with demonstrable criteria. The aim of the American system is to bring together in a separate legal mechanism all those aspects of the planning process which have to do with private development. By determining the location and standards of private development, it aims to reconcile those conflicts of private interest which under the British system are settled on an ad hoc basis in the general context of the development plan. Does it in fact result in greater consistency and less contention?

There is very little available evidence on which to judge the efficacy of the American system. The only published study of the subject was prepared by the Philadelphia Bureau of Municipal Research in 1955 for the Philadelphia Zoning Advisory Commission which was revising the city's zoning ordinance. The report found that the original ordinance, adopted in 1933, had been amended over a thousand times by the city council. Since 1933, the Board of Zoning Adjustment had granted approximately 35,000 variances and 3,500 exceptions (roughly speaking, a variance relates to a detailed dimensional control and an exception to a land-use control). The net result was that about 5 percent of the properties in the city (population around two million) were not in strict compliance with the zoning ordinance, excluding those not in compliance when the original ordinance was enacted. This hardly seems excessive; indeed if the zoning system was adequate in 95 percent of cases, it would be a remarkable achievement. But the zoning ordinance was very limited in scope compared with more recent revisions, and had never been strictly enforced. There were undoubtedly many thousand more unauthorized exceptions. The lack of a comprehensive development plan for the city made the exercise of control onerous and uncertain. In these circumstances the Board of Adjustment had to overcome as best it could the deficiencies of controls that were out of date and limited in scope. In 1956 the Board granted 2,585 variances and exceptions out of 3,813 heard—roughly two in three.

Whatever the planning implications of the Board's decisions, the figures show the volume of appeals produced by such a system. It is generally found that a revised ordinance does not reduce the number of appeals appreciably, since although the land-use controls may be better related to existing conditions, the introduction of far more detailed controls creates many more occasions for appeal.

A detailed breakdown of the cases before the Philadelphia Board in four hearings shows the types of cases dealt with (Table IV).

Of the 256 cases, only thirty were heard with the appellants present (although they were allowed to attend in all cases), and these took over 40 percent of the Board's time. The average time spent on a case without the appellant present was 3½ minutes, and 18 minutes when the appellant attended.

Table IV   Cases Heard by Philadelphia Board of Zoning Adjustment. 11 September–2 October 1956

Cases heard	256
Appeals granted	143
Granted with conditions	49
Refused	47
Withdrawn, etc.	17
Type of use involved	
1. Multifamily dwellings	43%
2. Other residential	7%
3. Special permits	17%
4. Commercial uses not in residential areas	11%
5. Commercial uses or home occupations in residential areas	15%
6. Industrial uses—all districts	6%
7. Miscellaneous	1%
	100%

In 1956 a revised procedure was introduced and a new Board appointed. I was present at one day's hearings. The Board dealt with fifty cases in five hours. All appellants attended the hearings, but procedure was very poor. Each applicant and his supporters stood before a large table, facing the six-member Board who sat on a magistrate's type bench. All hearings began with a request to the applicant to identify the site and explain what he wanted to do. Most applicants were represented by a lawyer, but the Board usually addressed questions to the applicant. Photos are required of each site, and if they are not available the case is deferred. Applicants must show proof of interest in the property (e.g., deeds), but this can be a contract of sale subject to the result of the appeal. Members of city departments may be asked to attend and answer questions, but the lack of proper procedural rules results in confused evidence: the one such witness called stood among a large group of objectors and a free-for-all debate ensued. Objectors attended in two or three cases, but were similarly confused by the disorderly procedure; there was no adequate opportunity to question witnesses or appellants.

The Board issues a decision within ten days of the hearing. The vote is recorded and available for inspection, but the Board gives no reason for the decision unless the case is taken to the courts on appeal. No report of the proceedings is issued. The Board may attach conditions to consent and may give temporary permissions renewable on a yearly basis.

At the hearing I attended, of the twenty-four cases heard in the afternoon session, only one was of any substance. This involved a proposal for a coin-operated laundramat (27 washers, 8 driers) to be open twenty-four hours a day seven days a week without supervision in a residence district. It was so obvious that this would be denied that to bring it was a waste of time and money. The Board had evidently made known its dislike of these businesses, and there was legislation before the city council to bring them under stricter regulation. The rest of the cases were very minor in character—mostly conversions of older properties to multi-family use or small-scale manufacturing uses (one-man industries) in commercial zones. Several were to regularize long-standing nonconformance brought to light by recent code enforcement.

The system seemed to work reasonably well and expeditiously in dealing with minor adaptations of the controls to fit particular cases. But most of the cases were so trivial as to be well within the scope of the most cautious administrative discretion and not remotely worth the attention of a well-paid and distinguished citizen board.

A study of cases before the Board of Zoning Adjustments in New Orleans brings into focus another aspect of the appeal machinery. This report was prepared by the Planning Commission staff on instructions from the City Council and has now been made public (1960). The report covered 963 cases considered by the Board between January 1958 and January 1960. The findings were summarized as follows:

1. Of 963 cases studied, 863 or 89.6% were granted.
2. Of 863 cases granted, 329 are considered by the Commission and by the Department of Law to be outside the authority of the Board.
3. The Commission considers that 220 cases granted on the basis of alleged hardship did not constitute a hardship under the terms and definition thereof contained in the Zoning Ordinance.
4. Of the 863 cases granted, 314 fully met all requirements, spirit, and intent of the law and were properly granted.

Several planning directors told me that probably a good third of permits issued by the building inspector's department are illegal. But this apparent flouting of the law is attributable as much to the rigid, legalistic character of the controls as to excessive laxity in their administration. One has considerable sympathy with the New Orleans Board's reply to the Planning Commission's report.

It has been called to the attention of this Board that the many cases granted by the Board tend to weaken the Zoning Ordinance. It is the Board's opinion that to the contrary, unless cases were granted by this Board, which has been considered since its creation the 'safety valve' of the Zoning Ordinance, the strict application of the law in many cases would produce practical difficulties and unnecessary hardships.
The Board in granting the numerous cases has felt that it was performing a community good and in many cases was of the opinion that the grants made covered 'better planning' than if the strict application of the Ordinance were adhered to.

An analysis of the 963 cases dealt with by the Board shows the type of situation in which standardized zoning controls may cause inconvenience (Table V):

Table V   Cases heard by New Orleans Board of Zoning Adjustment. 1958–1960

Lot area per family	20%
Yard variances	63%
Alterations and/or extensions, non-conforming uses	4%
Off-street loading or parking	9%
Height limitations	1%
More than one principal residential use on single lot	2%
Zoning district line adjustment	1%

Obviously the reasonableness of such petitions is a matter of degree, but probably the great majority, as in Philadelphia, were of a very minor order. The main defect of the system is not that it requires occasional adaptations, but that this process should entail the paraphernalia of appeal and quasi-judicial review. And that is attributable not to the system but to American distrust of bureaucratic authority.

Apart from triviality, the worst aspect of the appeal machinery is the lack of proper procedure for the conduct of hearings. After attending several public hearings before various agencies, I formed the impression that the American version of the process is usually farcical and always unsatisfactory as a means either of getting at the facts or simply ventilating public opinion. The procedure usually embarrasses the Board or impedes the appellants or both. Two reasons were given me for this democratic paradox: one was that the American public never accepts a governmental decision as final, and if controversy is sustained there will always be another so-called "public hearing"; the other reason is the related one that there is usually the possibility of appeal to the more orderly and thorough review of the courts.

Despite the vast number of appeals for variances and amendments, comparatively few find their way to the courts. In 1953 there were 248 zoning cases recorded in the standard law reports. Of these, 118 were decided by the highest state courts; three states, New York, New Jersey, and Pennsylvania, account for over half (130) of the cases reported (but this may have been due to better reporting of lower court cases in Pennsylvania).

The scope for judicial review of administrative or legislative action is by no means clear-cut. As explained in Part IV, it is comparatively easy to find grounds on which to bring cases before the court, but the grounds on which the court may reverse the decision are more limited. Apart from straight points of law or constitutionality, the appellant must show that the authority acted unreasonably. The Illinois Supreme Court in 1956 stated the oft-repeated principle that "To overcome the presumption of validity, it is incumbent upon the property owner to prove by clear and affirmative evidence that the restriction is arbitrary and unreasonable." In 1949 the Connecticut Supreme Court put it even more succinctly: "A court is without authority to substitute its own judgment for that vested by the statutes in a zoning authority."

There is some evidence that the courts are increasingly less willing to become a general reviewing agency in planning matters, and are disposed to allow the duly appointed authority, whether the city council or the Board of Appeals, to exercise final judgment. Between January 1954 and May 1957, the Illinois Supreme Court decided thirty zoning cases. In twenty-three of these the court upheld the validity of the ordinance, and in nine it reversed the decision of the lower court. The U.S. Supreme Court, since the early test cases of 1926 and 1928, has steadily declined to pass judgment in zoning cases. During the six terms 1949/1950 to 1954/1955 the Court dismissed appeals without comment or denied petitions for certiorari in twenty-one cases involving local planning matters. The inclination of the courts is to find that land-use control is essentially a local matter and capable of being resolved locally; only in cases of clear injustice will they intervene.

But the courts do play a very important role in shaping the general character and scope of land-use control by their function in reviewing the constitutionality of new techniques and application of established methods to new circumstances. From the early cases which established the validity of the zoning device, the courts have, despite some reverses from time to time, supported the gradual extension of land-use controls. And in so doing they have developed a rather remarkable body of jurisprudence relating to the proper scope of planning as a function of government and the effect of such controls on traditional concepts of property. I cannot possibly attempt to summarize this philosophy; it is reflected in the methods and attitudes described in this report. In America, it has always been the lawyers rather than the planners who have shouldered the intellectual burden of developing a theory of land-use control.[1] The result of the dominance of the courts in this process is that the controls cannot be readily extended or adapted to meet the needs or policy of the government of the day. Essentially they are evolved by judicial, not legislative, action. With the introduction of many new techniques and their adaptation to more purposeful planning policies, the courts will soon enter a crucial period in the history of planning law. Their decisions may well determine whether the public control of land use in America will be adequate to the needs of the next thirty years.

1. See the account in Part VII of the American Law Institute's current work on the drafting of a Model Land Development Code.

VI   CONCLUSION—1960

Reflections on the American System of Land-Use Control

It is hardly more than a historical accident, a singularly fortunate one, that there is any system of land-use controls available to American communities today. The controls which exist had their origin in the 1920's, the golden age of free enterprise and speculation in land. They received their judicial vindication in courts which reflected those attitudes. Their relationship to planning objectives was never so carefully considered by the lawyers who created them as their relationship to traditional concepts of private property. The many zoning ordinances adopted in 1921–31 were often poorly drafted and with a very limited concept of the public interest that they were supposed to serve. The wise use of land and the orderly development of the community were little considered, beyond the elementary principle of separating grossly incompatible uses, and even that extended only to the best neighborhoods. Many of these ordinances, enlarged and amended, are still in force, and the whole conception of land-use control in America is still greatly influenced by this parentage. There has been no radical departure. It is in the very nature of these controls that they leave an almost indelible impression on the pattern of land use, on judicial concepts of property and on public and political attitudes toward the question of land-use planning. Nevertheless, there has been over the past twenty years a gradual process of innovation and enlargement as individual communities have succeeded in bringing new types of control under the firmly established powers of zoning and subdivision regulation. Gradually these powers have been strengthened and extended as new techniques have developed. The cumulative effect was hard to judge until quite recently, when a number of cities embarked on thoroughgoing revision of their zoning system and an opportunity was given for sifting all the innovations and building the most useful into a new structure of control. The family

106

resemblance between the latest zoning ordinances and the earliest is certainly very marked, and it is unreasonable to look for any dramatic change in the impact of these new controls on the urban scene. Land-use controls can seldom do much to alter the existing state of things. But their influence on the rebuilding of American cities that is now getting under way may be very significant. Similarly, their contribution in shaping the living conditions of the vast population increase expected in the next twenty years could be vitally important and wholly beneficial.

But there are three obstacles facing the future progress toward more coherent and effective use of land-use controls in America.

The first of these obstacles is the impatience of many American planners themselves with the whole system of zoning, which many of them seem to regard as an incubus to be thrown off before there can be any real progress in planning. For some city planners it is an impatience born of despair at ever getting a satisfactory revision of their inherited controls passed by the city council. Yet New York and Chicago have shown that it can be done, and no city could be faced with a greater burden of revision or more formidable political situation. Others despair of zoning ever being an effective instrument while its very methods and administration lay it open to so much abuse and manipulation. But this is a reflection on the standards of American city government, not on the system of control itself. Subdivision controls are widely regarded as a more promising field for future planning purposes than zoning, but this is very largely because they are generally administered by the planning commission and its staff rather than by the city council (which, in turn, is regarded by some as an "undemocratic" state of affairs). There is no inherent reason why zoning and subdivision control should be treated as separate systems or why the controls contained in one system should be more effective than those contained in the other. A further reason for some planners' impatience is that they see, or think they see, just beyond their reach a vast armory of controls and other methods of influencing private development in comparison with which the traditional methods seem ridiculously cumbersome and inadequate. The dictatorial powers exercised by some directors of urban renewal (who, with a golden site in their pocket, can make developers dance to any tune they care to play) may well make the average city planning director despair at the limited scope of the powers at his disposal. But it is no good for American planners to hope for any sudden edict from above which will vastly strengthen and extend their powers, while sweeping away traditional controls. Those controls are here to stay, and the future will have to be built on them.

Zoning, in short, is not the Achilles' heel of American planning, as some critics have recently been complaining. Together with subdivision control, it is the main hope for the future. Many practicing planners in local government have shown that with skill and determination a more flexible and effective instrument can be fashioned from these powers. It would help matters forward if the academic planners would take more interest in these practical matters.

The second obstacle to progress toward more purposeful land-use controls in America is the growing demand from some critics of the zoning system for even greater precision and certainty in these controls and the reduction of all planning policies to controls of common application, including specific exceptions to the general controls. In all these recent discussions, the dominant theme is the insistence on common standards, since such standards are as much a check on the arbitrary action of the planning authority as on the quality of development. But while it is all very well to demand that a developer should be able to know what he can do with his property, the fact is that the developer is often the only person who *does* know what he can do with his property. Certainly he is the only person who knows what he would like to do with it, and what precisely is involved in his proposals. To insist on building into the zoning regulations an elaborate structure of standards may grossly limit the initiative of the developer. The main defect of the older zoning ordinances was that the standards they specified became increasingly obsolete and inimical to social and technical

changes. The legalistic insistence on precision in standards may run directly counter to the search for more effective controls which is just beginning to bear fruit. Instead
of adapting control more effectively to the needs of orderly
growth and instead of serving the legitimate interests of the
private developer, it may result in an even more inflexible
system than the original. Nor are standardized controls,
however impeccable from the lawyer's point of view, likely
to win general acceptance in America if at the same time
they narrow the scope for enterprise and place unnecessary
restraints on the forces of growth.

The dangers of discrimination and monopoly are also inherent in the insistence on more specific standards. The
debate on the Wayne Township case drew out the fallibility
of arguments based on minimum standards. But there are
other dangers, too. One is that all developers who can meet
the required standards would be allowed to develop, and
the blighting effects of overcompetition will emerge. This is
particularly relevant to the problem of the large suburban
shopping center. It is no part of land-use controls in a free
enterprise economy to shelter the developer from the effects
of a competitive situation, but the effect on the amenities
of a neighborhood may be fairly catastrophic. The other
danger is that under the traditional system the developer
sets his own standards within the districts allocated to his
type of use, whereas when the authority sets standards of
general application it may (a) increase prices, (b) prevent
new ideas and methods, as statutory specification usually
does, (c) provide a far more irksome and detailed application of control, and (d) afford still further opportunities for
misuse or compromise.

What is needed is less emphasis on *standards* (which relate to methods) and more emphasis on *policies* (which relate to objectives). A clear statement of the principles on
which the exercise of control is based and the objectives
which it is intended to serve, can be just as effective in
eliminating discriminatory practices (and provides a sounder
basis for judicial review) but at the same time can afford
much greater scope for initiative and allow control to adapt

more readily to the needs of changing circumstance and the unpredictable. In this view the system of control ceases to be a static set of standards related to a fixed pattern of land use and becomes a process progressively developing as the unknown factors which shape a community's growth reveal themselves. Standards remain an important part of such a system, but they are governed by stated policies, and are used as guides rather than as absolutes. The justification for specific standards is seldom self-evident. If challenged in court, they have to be justified on a rational basis, and even sound arguments may smack of expediency if there has been no earlier attempt to define the objectives involved.

For these reasons the most promising aspect of current thinking on problems of land-use control in America is not that which insists on ever more precise and specific types of control but that which seeks a more explicit statement of the public policies which the controls should implement. The exercise of control may then be judged not by its adherence to specific standards but by the extent to which it can be shown to further the overall objectives of community development. This approach calls for gathering relevant facts so that trends are early foreseen, for relating planning policies to the system of control, for articulating those policies and keeping them under review, and for the establishment of fair, open, and impartial procedures. The American planning profession, and the lawyers who proved themselves such effective allies in the early days of land-use control, will have to address themselves urgently to this subject if progress is to be maintained toward more effective and coherent land-use controls.

The third obstacle to future progress in American planning is the fact that while, during the past few years, more and more precise and restrictive land-use controls have been brought under the umbrella of the police power, there is still no obligation or even power to compensate owners for the losses incurred as a result of those controls. Such a situation cuts both ways: it may facilitate control since its exercise is not a charge on public funds, but it may also stultify control by imposing too heavy a penalty on private property. There comes a point in the exercise of control where the community is reluctant to require that the cost of public benefit should be borne entirely by private loss.

The success of land-use controls in America probably owes everything to the fact that they have cost the taxpayer nothing. A crucial question facing American planners and their legal strategists is whether the urgent need to grapple with the problems of the exploding metropolis and the aging city can be met only by new measures of control accompanied by compensation for damage to property rights and values. That would be a complete break with the traditional basis of American land-use controls, and some are prepared to argue that it is one which the affluent society should be prepared to take in the interests of a better environment. But apart from the practical obstacles to such a course (which would probably lead to pressure for compensating other types of control at present uncompensated, which in turn would certainly lead to the abandonment of control in most communities), the situation may not be so desperate. Given the facts and attitudes outlined earlier in this report, the need to exert substantially more stringent control over private development than is exercised by the more intelligent and farsighted planning authorities is not very apparent. Certain planning objectives, however, may well call for somewhat wider use of the powers of eminent domain in order to acquire specific advantages or rights for the public at large. But this could be achieved without destroying the established police-power basis of land-use controls.

My general impression, after talking with a great many planning officials and others, is that the powers available can be sufficiently effective in securing that degree of control over land use which American public opinion is prepared to accept, and which the courts are prepared to uphold as a valid use of the police power, and which perhaps falls less short of what the professional planner desires than he has been accustomed to assume.

Finally, what of the relevance of the American system

to planning in Britain? The American and British approaches to the problem of controlling private development represent almost the opposite extremes in planning methods. But the distinction between a formal system of regulatory controls, which eschews discretion as far as possible, and the alternative of exercising control as a discretionary power in government is perhaps more apparent than real. In both systems the power of control must be seen to be used fairly and effectively to further accepted public policies. It is in the choice of policies rather than in the choice of methods that real differences lie.

In America, public planning policies as they are understood in Britain have hardly begun to emerge and certainly never pass beyond the confines of individual municipalities.[1] The principal objective of American controls remains the traditional protection of private property interests. Such objectives as the long-term programming of private development, reservation of land for future public use, prevention of piecemeal redevelopment in areas which will later be subject to comprehensive redevelopment, and protection of undeveloped land for its agricultural, recreational, or landscape value are generally beyond the scope of present controls and are only rarely admitted as proper or necessary objectives of public policy.

I am by no means convinced that American control methods are totally inadequate to more purposeful planning policies, but few cities which I visited had an up-to-date and comprehensive (or credible) plan for land use and future development, and very few had attempted to state their policies for control of land use in any but the most cursory manner. Such genuine planning work as was done was mostly on public development; there might be a very competent plan for health centers, highways, or fire stations, but it seems rather futile to tackle the parts before the whole. If there were such a comprehensive plan and a written statement of objectives, one would be better able to assess the adequacy of the methods. As it is, one has to approach the methods through the historical perspective of

1. There are signs of change. See Part VII.

their origin and their function as an instrument of resolving conflicts of private interest in the use of land. But I believe that this itself is instructive for the British observer, because we have persistently averted our eyes from the fact that the "public interest" which we believe planning serves is sometimes a quite narrow private interest. The American system makes much more explicit the motives which underlie disputes about land use.

In Britain, however, the planning policies which have been evolved in the past twenty years, and those which will be essential if we are to survive as an industrial country with high living standards while at the same time preserving all that is best in British landscape and architecture, require that government shall exercise the decisive influence over private development. The system of financial compensation that has been adopted and the fundamental change in property rights effected by the 1947 Act mean that those policies can be carried out with a fair degree of consistency and success. It would be pointless to abandon the initiative which has passed to the public authorities in favor of a regulatory system which is appropriate where the initiative still rests with the private developer.

VII RETROSPECT AND PROSPECT—1969

Ten Years Later

In this part I attempt to review the more significant developments that have taken place in the field of land-use controls in America over the ten years since my original report (the preceding six parts) was written and to point to some parallels with the British experience.

Perhaps the most significant change that has occurred in America over the past decade has been a growing public awareness of the problems of the urban environment and a growing demand for greater public participation in the planning process.

In Part I of my report I noted that "it is very rare in America to encounter any antipathy to new development." That is probably still broadly true, in the sense that the American tradition is to welcome growth and change, not to resist it. In the ideology, new development is proof of prosperity. At the local level, as I showed elsewhere in the report, land-use controls are predicated largely on the protection of property values and are often used to prevent or exclude certain types of development (trailer camps, apartment blocks, Chinese laundries) that are regarded as disruptive of established property values. But the controls are designed to regulate the type of development permitted, not to prevent development of all kinds.

The traditional controls can be, and have been, used effectively to guide and regulate new private development. What is now happening is that the public are finding that the control of private development is not in itself enough to ensure the protection of property values, and that the Chinese laundry is not the only, or even the most alarming, threat to the American suburban heritage. In an address to the Federal Bar Association in December 1968, Richard F. Babcock urged his audience to realize that they were faced with "a pervasive public outcry over the deterioration of our physical environment . . . a concern over the condition

114

of our air and water, a sensitivity to visual amenities, a demand for preservation of historical landmarks"—and that these were now political facts to be reckoned with. The conference was concerned with national energy policy, and Babcock warned that "the impact of utility facilities upon the neighborhood is a cost that will be included in any calculus of the cost-benefit of a proposal for expansion."

It is interesting to find that in some areas local communities have turned to zoning controls as a means of controlling the unwelcome intrusion of public utility development. In 1965 the Court of Appeals of Maryland sustained the requirement of the Baltimore County Board of Zoning Appeals that Baltimore Gas and Electric Company place transmission lines underground through a residential area, at an additional cost of nearly a million dollars. Whether this extension of local zoning controls to public utility development, with its inherent conflict with the statutory powers and duties of such undertakings, will be sustained remains to be seen.

In Britain we have witnessed a similar recrudescence of public concern over the control of development by utilities (statutory undertakers) and other public authorities. Although public bodies are generally required to comply with control procedures, there are inevitably cases where the necessities of public development bring it into conflict with implacable local objections. Experience has shown that public opinion will not be reconciled to such development in any case where the decision to develop, however rational, has been arrived at in a way which appears to lack formality ("due process") or which does not afford adequate opportunity for those directly affected to object and to have their objections heard. The leading case was the government's decision to locate a third international airport at Stanstead in rural Essex. As a result of the pressure of public opinion the issue was subsequently referred to a specially appointed commission under Mr. Justice Roskill. The president of the Board of Trade, in appointing the commission, directed its attention to the following matters which were of special relevance to its inquiry: "General planning issues, including population and employment growth, noise, amenity, and effect on agriculture and existing property; aviation issues, including air traffic control and safety; surface access; defence issues; and cost, including the need for cost/benefit analysis." Provisions were also introduced into the new Town and Country Planning Act 1968 to enable similar cases in future to be referred to Planning Inquiry Commissions separately appointed for each reference.[1]

In his address to the Federal Bar Association, Richard Babcock warned his audience that "We are living in an era marked by a growing demand by the citizen for participation in decisions that he believes affect his interests. This is true whether you are talking about the ghetto, the university or the posh suburbs of Westchester County and Chicago's North Shore."

This recent escalation of demand for public participation in planning is very striking, both in America and in Britain. In neither country is it yet possible to assess its potential impact, but it is clear that the public are no longer content to leave planning in the hands of the professional planners and that the demand for participation arises from a conviction that the planning process is not sufficiently responsive to local interests and public opinion. Similarly, neither country has yet succeeded in evolving effective means of securing public participation in planning.

The present situation was brilliantly depicted in a cartoon by R. Hedman on the cover of the September 1968 issue of the *Journal of the American Institute of Planners*.[2] This shows the city planning department at the center, with its planners enmeshed in cobwebs, poring over the 1923 Master Plan, stymied by an econometric model and dreaming inconsequential dreams. Around this Rip van Winkle establishment charge a variety of citizen groups vigorously par-

1. See Town and Country Planning Act 1968, Sections 61–63. The Planning Inquiry Commissions would not themselves decide the case but would take evidence, hear objections, examine alternative sites and report to the Minister.
2. Vol. XXXIV (September 1968).

ticipating and carrying banners shouting "Action Now," "Social Change," "A New Order," "Revolt," "New Directions," and, simply, "Wow!"

Ten years ago planners in many American cities were struggling to arouse public interest in planning. They seem to have released a juggernaut. In America the democratic tradition is still strong, and no one denies the right of all members of the community to be heard in matters affecting the community's life and development. American planners and social scientists are responding in a variety of ways to this demand for grass roots democracy in the planning process. In the same (September 1968) issue of the *Journal of the American Institute of Planners,* Edmund M. Burke, Chairman of Community Organization and Social Planning at the Boston Graduate School of Social Work, published an article on "Citizen Participation Strategies," in which he analyzed "the basic conflicts between participatory democracy and professional expertise."[3] He noted that planners and "other urban professionals" had encountered many problems in attempting to encourage citizen participation in community decision making. He suggested that some of these dilemmas could be resolved by "recognizing and adopting a strategy of participation specifically designed to fit the role and resources of the particular organization." He then goes on to identify five types of strategies: "education-therapy, behavioral change, staff supplement, cooptation, and community power"—which is enough to give any of us pause for thought.

At the other end of the spectrum are some ideas put forward on the same subject by James V. Cunningham, Lecturer in Urban Organizing, Graduate School of Social Work, University of Pittsburgh, in an address to the 1968 ASPO National Planning Conference, on "Absentee Planning and the Integrated Society." He sees the role of the planner as much more that of a social worker than as the technician responsible for producing physical plans and standards of development which, he argues, may have little relevance to

3. *Ibid.* pp. 287–294.

the realities of community life and aspirations. He suggests that the alternative to master planning would be "to supply neighborhoods with their own local planner in residence, housed in a convenient storefront, working intimately with the people of the area, answerable to an elected neighborhood board." He remarks that "It is ironic that the question even has to be raised of public planners learning to have an intimate client relationship with the people of a neighborhood." In conclusion he states his belief that "all of us involved in planning can contribute to the making of a single peaceful integrated society—but it will come from what we are and how we establish our relations with people in cities much more than from the physical standards we apply."[4]

Well outside these two extremes of the theoretical and the earthy approach to citizen participation, Daniel P. Moynihan has been sounding a skeptical warning from the viewpoint of the political scientist. Shortly after his appointment as President Nixon's adviser on urban affairs, Dr. Moynihan published a study of the practical results of the community action programs initiated in New York under the Federal Government's Economic Opportunity Act 1964. This act required "maximum feasible participation of the residents of the areas and the members of the groups" involved in the program. Dr. Moynihan's views are succinctly stated in the title of his book *Maximum Feasible Misunderstanding.*[5] He characterizes the results of the community action programs as "soaring rhetoric, minimum performance."

Nevertheless, the demand for public participation in planning cannot be balked, and it is not enough merely to afford the public an opportunity to object to the plans that the planners produce. Participation, if it is not simply to formalize the conflict between planners and the public, must en-

4. *Planning 1968* (Chicago: American Society of Planning Officials, 1968), pp. 178–183.

5. The Free Press, New York (1968).

sure that the public is able to take part both in the formulation of plans and in their implementation.

In Britain there has been a similar concern to provide for public participation in planning. The new Town and Country Planning Act 1968[6] introduces a major change in the centralized system established by the 1947 Act, whereby all development plans had to be submitted to the minister for approval. The new act provides for two levels of plan making, "structure plans," which deal with the general strategy for future development and redevelopment (including integrated planning for land use and traffic) and which are still required to be submitted to the Minister for approval; and second, "local plans" which apply the general strategies of the structure plans in detail to particular areas. These local plans are not submitted to the Minister for approval. For both structure plans and local plans the new Act requires the local planning authority to give publicity to the matters which they propose to include in the plan and to take account of any representations made by members of the public on these proposals *before* they proceed to prepare the plan. When the plan has been prepared, members of the public again have an opportunity to make objections to it, and these objections are heard at a public local inquiry. In the case of structure plans the inquiry is held by an inspector appointed by the Minister, but in the case of local plans the inspector may be appointed either by the Minister or, in certain cases, by the local planning authority themselves. The authority are required to consider any such objections before formally adopting a local plan, either as originally prepared or as modified so as to take account of objections or any matters arising out of those objections.

It has yet to be seen how this new planning system, which provides both for greater public participation *and* greater

6. For the background to this act, see the report of the Planning Advisory Group on *The Future of Development Plans* (London: Her Majesty's Stationery Office, 1965) and the White Paper *Town and Country Planning*, Cd. 3333 (London: Her Majesty's Stationery Office, 1967).

autonomy for the local planning authority, will work out in practice. A departmental committee chaired by Mr. Arthur Skeffington, Joint Parliamentary Secretary at the Ministry of Housing and Local Government, was appointed in 1968 "To consider, and to report . . . on the best methods, including publicity, of securing participation of the public at the formative stage in the making of development plans for their area." The committee's report is awaited.

It will be extremely interesting to see how the demand for public participation in the planning process is worked out in our two countries. We have been accustomed to the truism that planning is for people. But that "for" is symptomatic: planning was something done *for* people. Planners now have to come to terms with planning *by* people.

It was, no doubt, largely as a result of public concern about the problems of the urban environment, that President Johnson in 1965, after years of pressure from professional planners and a succession of defeats for the proposal in Congress, established the Department of Housing and Urban Development (HUD). For the first time, housing and planning were represented at Cabinet level—and incidentally, by the first Negro American to be appointed to Cabinet rank, Robert C. Weaver. The achievement of Cabinet status came some seventy years after the U.S. Congress made its first recorded appropriation for dealing with the problems of urban development, when in 1892 it voted $20,000 for the Secretary of Labor to investigate slums in cities of over 200,000 population. In 1967 HUD programs were supporting annually about $12 billion in public and private investments in housing and urban development.

It is not my purpose to attempt to describe the extent of HUD's activities. Those who are interested in its origin and scope will find a full account of them in John B. Williams' volume in the Praeger Library of U.S. Government Departments and Agencies.[7] The need for a new integrated Depart-

7. John B. Williams *The Department of Housing and Urban Development* (New York: Praeger, 1967).

ment to deal with the massive complex of urban problems was eloquently expressed by President Johnson in his message to Congress on March 2, 1965:

This new Department will provide a focal point for thought and innovation and imagination about the problems of our cities . . . it will work to strengthen the constructive relationships between nation, state and city—the creative federalism—which is essential to progress. This partnership will demand the leadership of mayors, Governors and state legislatures . . . .

We have over nine million homes, most of them in cities, which are run down or deteriorating; over four million do not have running water or even plumbing. Many of our central cities are in need of major surgery to overcome decay. New suburban sprawl reaches out into the countryside, as the process of urbanization consumes a million acres a year. The old, the poor, the discriminated against are increasingly concentrated in central city ghettos, while others move to the suburbs, leaving the central city to battle against immense odds.

Physical decay, from obsolescent schools to polluted water and air, helps breed social decay. It casts a pall of ugliness and despair on the spirits of the people. And this is reflected in rising crime rates, school dropouts, delinquency and social disorganization.

HUD incorporates a variety of former federal departments and agencies, including the Housing and Home Finance Agency (HHFA), the Federal Housing Administration (FHA), the Federal Home Loan Bank (FHLB), the Federal National Mortgage Association ("Fanny Mae"), the Public Housing Administration (PHA), the Urban Renewal Administration (URA), and the Community Facilities Administration (CFA). For our purposes, the most significant component of the new Department was the creation of two new divisions under the Assistant Secretary for Metropolitan Development and the Assistant Secretary for Demonstrations and Intergovernmental Relations.

The Assistant Secretary for Metropolitan Development is responsible for programs affecting urban areas and their hinterland, including programs dealing with metropolitan and urban planning, water and sewer facilities, the acquisition of recreational open space and the preservation of natural beauty, urban mass transportation and research, and planned community development. The division disposes of a formidable armory of federal grants (mainly on a matching basis with monies raised from state and local sources) and loans designed as incentives to secure better urban planning, coordinated metropolitan planning, the advance acquisition of land to be reserved for public uses, the preservation of open space, "urban beautification," research and demonstration programs on mass transportation, and the development of public works programs. The division is concerned primarily with the promotion of better and more comprehensive planning for the metropolitan areas and the closely related work of transportation research, including applied research in the actual testing of new methods of urban transit. This side of its work is brilliantly illustrated in its 1968 report on the study of new systems for urban transportation.[8]

As head of the Metropolitan Development Division, Assistant Secretary Charles M. Haar was able to take positive action to promote the preparation of up-to-date, comprehensive, and technically competent master plans without which, as he had insisted in his earlier writings while at the Harvard Law School, land-use controls are either arbitrary or ineffective or both.[9] Speaking in his new role Haar said:

We know we are going to have to build an urban America in the next 35 years equal to all we have built since Jamestown. The question now is, what is it going to look like: and how can all citizens be given more of a choice of where and how they want to live? The initiative is with the local area to develop its own plan—a plan that is consistent with other over-all planning involving the locality.

8. *Tomorrow's Transportation—New Systems for the Urban Future:* U.S. Department of Housing and Urban Development, Washington, D. C., 1968.

9. See Haar, *The Master Plan: An Impermanent Constitution, Law and Contemporary Problems,* Vol. 20, 353–380 (1955).

The other new division set up in HUD, under the Assistant Secretary for Demonstrations and Intergovernmental Relations, is responsible for administering the Model Cities program enacted by the Demonstration Cities and Metropolitan Development Act 1966.[10] This program has attracted much interest and it is worth setting out the Title I Findings and Declaration of Purpose as an indicator of the planning problems which concern America and which are so much more clearly recognized now than they were ten years ago:

Sec. 101. The Congress hereby finds and declares that improving the quality of urban life is the most critical domestic problem facing the United States. The persistence of widespread urban slums and blight, the concentration of persons of low income in older urban areas, and the unmet needs for additional housing and community facilities and services arising from rapid expansion of our urban population have resulted in a marked deterioration in the quality of the environment and the lives of large numbers of our people while the Nation as a whole prospers.

The Congress further finds and declares that cities, of all sizes, do not have adequate resources to deal effectively with the critical problems facing them, and that Federal assistance in addition to that now authorized by the urban renewal program and other existing Federal grant-in-aid programs is essential to enable cities to plan, develop, and construct programs to improve their physical environment, increase their supply of adequate housing for low and moderate-income people, and provide educational and social services vital to health and welfare.

The purposes of this title are to provide additional financial and technical assistance to enable cities of all sizes (with equal regard to the problems of small as well as large cities) to plan, develop, and carry out locally prepared and scheduled comprehensive city demonstration programs containing new and imaginative proposals to rebuild or revitalize large slum and blighted areas; to expand housing, job, and income opportunities; to reduce the incidence of crime and delinquency; to enhance recreational and cultural opportunities; to establish better access between homes and jobs; and generally to improve living condi-

10. Public Law 89–754.

tions for the people who live in such areas, and to accomplish these objectives through the most effective and economical concentration and coordination of Federal, State, and local public and private efforts to improve the quality of urban life.

The financial backing which the Model Cities program has won from Congress testifies to the urgency of the problems—$12 million in planning grants, $400 million in supplementary funds for the year ending June 30, 1968, and $250 million in grants for urban renewal projects in Model City neighborhoods.

Land-use controls find a modest but important part in the Model Cities program, since one of the requirements of eligibility for assistance under the program (as with the former "workable programs" under Section 701 of the Housing Act 1954 as amended) is that "substantive local laws, regulations, and other requirements are, or can be expected to be, consistent with the objectives of the program"—including effective zoning and subdivision controls.

It must be admitted that against the glamour of the new policies initiated under the auspices of the Metropolitan Development Division and the Model Cities Program, the traditional methods of land-use control look distinctly old-fashioned, not to say tatty. There is a danger that they will, as so often in the past, be ignored or taken for granted by those whose main concern is with the preparation of sophisticated, coordinated plans for metropolitan and urban development, or with the implementation of demonstration projects sustained by massive federal subventions. But, in the end, plans are no better than the means of implementing them, and demonstration projects will not generate lasting results unless an effective system for controlling development, and for code enforcement, exists.

It is important to note, therefore, that one of the duties of the Assistant Secretary for Demonstrations and Intergovernmental Relations is to supervise the code studies division of HUD and to make studies of housing and building codes, zoning regulations, and development standards.

The National Commission on Urban Problems has been asked to undertake a thorough review of these systems.[11]

Parallel with the intense governmental involvement in planning at the federal level through HUD, has been a revival of interest in the role of state governments as planning agencies. Although HUD has given financial backing to the Institute on State Programming for the 70's (which was set up in 1967 and is undertaking a nationwide survey on the status and effectiveness of planning in the fifty states) and has also extended some of its programs to state agencies, HUD is primarily concerned with urban and metropolitan planning and has not sought to promote the states as effective regional planning authorities.

It has always been something of a puzzle why the states have not developed their potential in the planning field. They have the powers of the legislature; they control major public works programs (such as interstate highways); they have the predominant interest in the conservation and allocation of natural resources, and they have a wider oversight of urban and rural development problems than any other component of local government. The power conflict between the state and city governments has no doubt prevented positive action by the states in the cities themselves, but there is far less effective resistance to state authority in the suburban and rural counties which constitute by far the larger area of most states. Despite their strong strategic position and the pressure of public demand for positive planning, particularly in the field of conservation and anti-pollution measures, the states have not responded to this opportunity. There are a few exceptions, notably New York State and Minnesota,[12] but the general position was summed

11. See Research Report No. 15 prepared for the Commission by Fred P. Bosseelman, *Alternatives to Urban Sprawl: Legal Guidelines for Governmental Action* (Washington, D. C., 1968). The report examines three methods of controlling urban development: planned development zones; compensation to owners whose property is affected by highly restrictive regulations; and public land acquisition.

12. The state of Hawaii is unique in that since 1957 a State Land Use Commission has been charged with the duty of classifying all the

up by the chairman of the Institute on State Programming, Jack M. Campbell, at the 1968 ASPO National Planning Conference as follows:[13]

The performance of state planning agencies is inconsistent and inadequate. Their programs and activities are, for the most part, not relevant to the decision-making process, and the state planning agencies are not discharging the full responsibilities assigned to them by legislative and executive authority. The fact is that at present state planning is simply not relevant to short or long term decision making.

Former Governor Terry Sanford of North Carolina has put the point more succinctly, "Few governors concern themselves with planning, for planning simply to help the next governor seems irrelevant to the everyday tasks that pile up in a busy governor's office." But he also recognized the potential of planning as a political instrument: "To be effective, planning must be at the governor's right hand. He is the only person with the power to bring agencies together, determine priorities, and smooth out conflicts. And he needs to get his information quickly and accurately."[14]

The significance of the states' involvement in planning, so far as the study of land-use controls is concerned, is partly that the states are potentially capable of becoming the planning policy maker and executant over vast areas of the country, where city government does not impinge but where much of the urban development of the next thirty years will take place; and also that the states are the legislative authority through which any major revision of the

land in the state into one of three classifications: "urban," "agriculture," and "conservation" (a fourth zone "rural," to include low-density residential, was added in 1963) and imposing use regulations within those districts. An account of the Hawaiian experience is given by Ira Michael Heyman in the *Journal of the American Institute of Planners*, Vol. XXX (August 1964), pp. 248–252.

13. See the action on "Trends in State Planning" in *Planning 1968* (Chicago: American Society of Planning Officers).

14. Terry Sanford, *Storm Over the States* (New York: McGraw-Hill, 1967), pp. 193–194.

enabling statutes for zoning and related planning controls will have to pass.

Raymond T. Olsen, director of the Minnesota State Planning Agency, summed up the present situation very neatly at the 1968 ASPO National Planning Conference:[15] "the federal government has a corner on the money, the states have a corner on legal authority, and local governments a corner on the unique problems." But I would add that all three share a corner on the future of land-use controls— the federal government in undertaking research on improved techniques and providing incentives to their adoption; the states in passing the enabling legislation and ex- tending the use of effective controls to the rural areas; and the local governments in applying them. It is doubtful whether any of the three has yet taken a strong enough initiative in revising the basic instruments of land-use control, without which the more sophisticated planning exercises that are now being undertaken at all three levels will not have much effect on what actually happens on the ground.

In Britain we have a similar problem of reconciling the requirements of effective regional and subregional planning with the anachronistic pattern of local government boundaries. Although the 1947 Planning Act made the counties and county boroughs the local planning authorities (rather than the 1400 odd District Councils who had planning powers under the 1932 Act) this still leaves 160 local planning authorities in England to deal with an area smaller than most American states. In the early 1960's, the national government took the initiative in undertaking a series of regional planning studies which were to provide a policy framework for the local planning authorities. In 1965 Regional Economic Planning Councils were set up by the new Department of Economic Affairs to assist in the formulation of regional plans and to advise on their implementation. They have no executive powers. More recently, a number of Passenger Transport Authorities have been set up to co-

15. "Trends in State Planning," in *Planning 1968* (Chicago: American Society of Planning Officers, 1968), p. 253.

ordinate and operate public transport facilities in the most densely populated parts of the country. Meanwhile a Royal Commission on local government was appointed to review the structure of local government. In their written evidence[16] to the Commission the Ministry of Housing and Local Government put the case for a top tier of some 30 to 40 major authorities, related to the physical and economic pattern of subregions, and which would be capable of planning on a subregional basis. At the time of writing the Royal Commission's report is awaited.

Amid the rapidly increasing public interest in planning issues and the rapidly extending governmental response to those pressures, planners have been asking themselves questions about the methods they use and their relevance to the problems with which they have to deal. The principal theme of my original report was to demonstrate how land-use controls in America owed, if not their origin, their survival to the fact that they effectively served private property interests rather than any clearly articulated planning policies. I stressed the need for more emphasis on principles and objectives, and less emphasis on uniformity and precision in the methods of control. In fact, that passage in the concluding part of the report was marred by a spectacular misprint which exactly reversed my meaning. It has been corrected in the present edition and it reads:

the most promising aspect of current thinking on problems of land-use control in America is not that which insists on ever more precise and specific types of control but that which seeks a more explicit statement of the public policies which the controls should implement.

I am not sure that I was not unduly optimistic in discerning a growing awareness of the need to articulate the planning policies which land-use controls should implement. I have not seen much evidence of this over the past ten

16. Published by Her Majesty's Stationery Office, London, 1967.

years. I have already commented on the striking public concern for the problems of the urban environment and the
central city. But there has been relatively little progress in
relating the techniques of land-use control to these emergent problems. Indeed there is a real danger, as there was
ten years ago, that those techniques will be dismissed as
irrelevant, or simply ignored. No one would claim that land-
use controls in themselves can solve the problems of the
urban environment or cope adequately with the pressures
of urban growth. But they are potentially part of the machinery for handling those problems—and, what is more,
if they are misused or allowed to atrophy they can positively add to those problems. They are partly responsible
for the present physical condition of urban America; they
can aid or hinder the integration of the urban community;
and they can be used to help meet the present and future
need for effective control of the living environment. It is
important therefore to consider the relationship between
those controls and the objectives of public policy.

As the 1968 ASPO Conference (which seems to have been
a vintage year) several sessions were devoted to an examination of Physical Planning Standards and Social Goals.[17]

Matthew B. M. Lawson, in a paper on the social implications of physical standards, commented that "As the years
have gone by, these standards have become entrenched almost as goals in themselves rather than as means to an
end." He observed that "physical planning standards often
seem to have more to do with functional organization and
efficiency, the promotion of development, aesthetic effects,
and the protection of property values than with the social
goal of promoting individual well-being." It is legitimate to
comment that if land-use controls succeeded in contributing
effectively to policies aimed at functional organization and
efficiency, the promotion of development (of the right kind,
in the right place), and aesthetic effects, they would be per-

17. See *Planning 1968* (Chicago: American Society of Planning Officers), pp. 174–178. The 1969 ASPO Conference, to be held in
Cincinnati, will include sessions on "development of sharper planning tools": it will be interesting to see what emerges.

forming highly valuable social functions. Land-use controls have these potential functions but, as Lawson recognizes,

We are much less sure today than city planners once were about the way physical planning standards affect people's lives. The connection is much more complex than once was thought. Nowadays, we would seldom expect to hear people say that simply by creating a satisfactory environment can we expect people to be happy and social ills to disappear. Man seems to have an infinite capacity for developing problems regardless of how good his surroundings are.

True, but the creation of a good environment may help to avoid other problems, and problems which are the more serious because they cannot be solved by individual effort but involve the will of the community. "What do you mean by a good environment?"—well, one in which avoidable social stresses are diminished and the individual's prospects of comfort and happiness are enhanced. Land-use controls and the physical planning standards which they embody are not a panacea for social ills. Planners will become impotent through despair if they fail to utilize the means at their disposal simply because they cannot, in themselves, cure all social ills. That is not to say, however, that planners (and the planned) should not scrutinize those controls and those standards to ascertain what values and objectives they embody, and whether those values and objectives are compatible with, and relevant to, the aims of social policy. To take the obvious example, do the controls applied to residential development tend to foster an integrated or a segregated society? To take a less obvious example, why are the environmental standards laid down for industrial areas generally so inferior to those for residential areas, when the worker spends at least as much of his active life in the one as in the other?

Allan B. Jacobs, Director of the San Francisco Department of City Planning, contributing to the same symposium, recognized that the standards embodied in traditional zoning ordinances were probably a pretty accurate reflection of what most people wanted, even if they could not achieve it:[18]

One is often surprised and usually chagrined at how accurately they [land-use controls] portray widely held and even cherished ideals. Indeed, when a push comes to a shove, it appears that the goals that might be achieved by the standards, and the standards alone—yes, the single family house on a large lot, on a quiet tree-lined street, with a school and shopping center not too far away, or the equivalent of this picture and all that this implies for various kinds of areas in the community—oftentimes remain goals that apply to residents of poverty and ghetto areas. The problem in terms of today's crisis is, too often, not the goals but the inability of a large and frustrated part of our community to achieve those goals.

But it is not enough that land-use controls should be employed simply as an alternative means of enforcing restrictive covenants. In Part V of my report I commented on the situation in Houston, Texas, the largest city in America that has no zoning ordinance and which relies instead on private deed restrictions. When ASPO held their 1967 conference in Houston, the city attorney, William A. Olson, gave a spirited account of how that essentially private system of regulating land use has become institutionalized:

In the absence of zoning, Houston sought another method to regulate the use of land and to maintain some degree of integrity of the residential neighborhood. It came up with municipal participation in the contractual rights of individuals—it now participates in the enforcement of private deed restrictions. Now this is not a substitute for zoning and, if compared with the over-all purpose and scope of zoning, it may not even be a good alternative. Zoning is comprehensive, citywide; deed restrictions are limited, having application only to a particular area or subdivision of the city. Nevertheless it is the only tool we have, and

18. "Physical Standards and Some Social Implications," *Planning 1968* (Chicago: American Society of Planning Officers), pp. 183–188.

we are using it.[19] In 1965 the Texas Legislature enacted a statute (Article 974a–1, V.T.C.S.) which enables the city to sue in court to enjoin or abate the violation of duly recorded restrictive covenants. The city's right to expend time and money on enforcing private contractual rights, however, has not gone unquestioned and is being challenged in the courts.

There is a danger that land-use controls may be relegated, in the minds of those who have to grapple with the problems of urban growth, to little more than a system of publicly administered private deed restrictions—what might be known to planning theologians as the Houston heresy. There is certainly a tendency among American planners, perhaps even more marked now than it was ten years ago, to neglect the basic methods of land-use control—basic, because they are the only generally available methods, other than the exercise of land acquisition powers, of plan implementation. Unless America is prepared to contemplate the public acquisition of all undeveloped land and all property which requires to be redeveloped, the traditional powers of land-use control, as interpreted by modern techniques, are the principal means of regulating the spontaneous processes of growth, change, and decay in the physical environment.

At the working level, the slow process of revising and extending the traditional methods of zoning control and subdivision regulation has continued. There have been relatively few important innovations in technique. The most interesting of these has been the adoption in several states (notably Minnesota and New York) of new legislation or amendments to the State Enabling Acts to permit "unit" or "cluster" developments, i.e., the development of larger residential areas of varied density and house types, together with provision for integral open space, etc. The aim has been to introduce a much needed element of flexibility into residential zoning, so as to break away from the uniform zoning of huge areas for single houses on quarter-, half-, or

19. "City Population in the Enforcement of Private Deed Restrictions," *Planning 1967* (Chicago: American Society of Planning Officers), pp. 266–270.

one-acre plots. This attempt to provide for variety, experiment, and imagination in speculative development was foreshadowed by the provision for "planned developments" noted in Part IV. The increased readiness of planning authorities to permit such developments no doubt owes much to the fact that the national Association of Home Builders and the Urban Land Institute, both of which represent the interests of private developers, themselves commissioned and published in 1965 model state enabling legislation and zoning provisions to facilitate this type of development.[20]

The interest by private developers in undertaking large-scale planned developments, designed to provide a greater variety of housing types and amenities than has been typical of private enterprise housing in the past, has been most strikingly demonstrated in the private enterprise "new towns" at Reston, Virginia, and Columbia, Maryland.

Reston was conceived as a relatively small residential community, with exceptionally lavish provision for leisure-time pursuits—sailing, golf, etc. It was also intended to provide for a variety of income groups. After a promising start, however, progress has been relatively slow and various difficulties have been encountered, not least the invasion of residents' privacy by the boards of sightseers that this development attracts during summer weekends.

A much more ambitious scheme is being promoted at Columbia, Maryland, where a genuine private enterprise new town is being developed for a population of some 100,-000 by 1980. A great deal of highly qualified professional expertise in the fields of planning, architecture, sociology, and estate development is being invested in this scheme which, if it proves to be a commercial and social success, could have an immense influence on the future pattern of urban development in America.[21]

20. *Legal Aspects of Planned Unit Residential Development with Suggested Legislation,* Technical Bulletin 52 (Washington, D. C.: Urban Land Institute, 1965). The model code has now been enacted, with modifications, in New Jersey and Pennsylvania.

21. See *A Sketch of the Planning-Building Process for Columbia, Maryland* by Morton Hoppenfeld, *Journal of the American Institute of Planners,* Vol. XXXIII (November 1967), pp. 398–409.

Columbia is also attracting much interest in Britain, where there is increasing emphasis on private enterprise participation in the development of new towns. Twelve new towns have been started in Britain since 1961, and there are now 27 new towns in the program: 20 in England, 2 in Wales, and 5 in Scotland.

In recent years, several states have undertaken reviews of the general laws and ordinances dealing with planning and land-use controls, and have passed amending legislation aimed at clarifying and codifying the accumulated legislative morass of the past thirty or forty years (e.g., Minnesota, Pennsylvania, Connecticut, New York). Others (e.g., Maryland in 1966 and Massachusetts in 1967) have embarked on the same formidable undertaking.

In the same direction of revising the established procedures, the American Society of Planning Officials published in 1966 a new edition of their standard model zoning ordinance.[22]

These various efforts, however, have been concerned chiefly with systematizing the inherited confusion of land-use controls, and grafting on some of the more recent technical innovations, rather than with any major overhaul of the system itself. An exception to this general trend, or rather the culmination of this endeavor to improve and rationalize land-use controls, is the undertaking by the American Law Institute of what Judge Goodrich described as "a critical examination and reworking of the law relating to public control of land use and land development." This is much the most encouraging and potentially significant development in the field of land-use controls in the past decade and warrants a full account of its progress to date.

This is a mammoth undertaking with a $500,000 grant from the Ford Foundation to the A.L.I. It has already been in progress for six years and preceded by a two-year preliminary

22. Fred H. Blair, Jr., and Ernest K. Bartley, *The Text of a Model Zoning Ordinance with Commentary* (Chicago: American Society of Planning Officers, 1966).

feasibility study undertaken by Richard Babcock, also with a grant from the Ford Foundation. In April 1968 the Council of the American Law Institute published for their members' annual meeting the Tentative Draft No. 1 of a Model Land Development Code, prepared by a team of reporters led by Allison Dunham of the University of Chicago Law School, with the assistance of an advisory committee chaired by Richard Babcock. The present draft is solely the work of the Reporters and has not been approved by the A.L.I.

The object of the exercise is to carry out a comprehensive review and restatement of planning law, and to produce a new enabling act which could replace the two model acts prepared in the 1920's by the Department of Commerce under the direction of Secretary (later President) Herbert Hoover: the Standard State Zoning Enabling Act first issued in 1922, and the Standard City Planning Enabling Act first prepared in 1926.

In their Introductory Memorandum the Reporters begin by facing up to the problem of defining the objectives of land development law in the broadest terms, and of elucidating the relationships between the methods of physical planning and social and economic objectives, to which I have already referred as causing much concern and misgiving among professional planners. It is heartening to find the American legal profession once again coming to the aid of the planners, as it did when the validity of land-use controls was first established in the 1920's, and charting the way ahead with lucidity and concision:

Land becomes urbanized and developed as a result of a host of decisions of the private owners of land area and of the governmental agencies empowered to develop or control land. A central purpose of land planning or land development law as we prefer to call it, is to control or influence these decisions so as to make the development and redevelopment of the space conform to patterns beneficial to society. It would be possible to have planning and planning law which is focussed primarily or directly on social and economic factors and not on land development . . . . (but) the planning with which this Code is concerned is that of planning the physical development of land: proper location and intensity of activities which use land, and the type, design and location of structures and facilities that serve these activities.

To state that physical development is emphasized is not to say that land planning ignores social and economic objectives. It is rather to state that land planning seeks to identify the physical factors which can influence significantly realization of social and economic objectives. Land planning results in programs or policies for physical development which maximizes the opportunity to realize social and economic objectives.[23]

Just as Alfred Bettman and his colleagues, in presenting the case for public control of private development to the Supreme Court in 1926, found it expedient to stress the analogy with traditional concepts of the common law of "nuisance," so the Reporters stress that their proposals are organized on the basis of two established assumptions: "that the residual power to make development decisions should be lodged with the owner be he private or public; (and) that the public interest is best served if the basic power to interfere with private development decisions is lodged with a unit of local government." Having thus (hopefully) re-assured orthodox opinion that their approach has been essentially evolutionary not revolutionary, the Reporters proceed to outline the principles upon which they have conducted their review.

They begin by recognizing that there has grown up a wide range of governmental powers to influence land-use decisions, including such powers as building, fire, and health regulations, property taxes, tax exemptions, grants-in-aid, and public land acquisition. They comment that these various devices have been poorly integrated with land-use controls, and that all such methods should be brought within the scope of a comprehensive review. In the event, however, they conclude that "Logic at this point must yield to history, experience, time and financial resources," and that, while these related powers should be taken into account in

23. *Tentative Draft No. 1, Model Land Development Code* (Chicago: University of Chicago Law School, 1968).

considering the scope and methods of land-use controls, the practical approach is to limit the land development code to those powers which bear most directly on coordinating the physical development of the community—that is, the preparation of land-use plans, the regulation of land use, and the exercise of powers of eminent domain (compulsory purchase of land). In short "The basic legal issues in this project concern the sanctions and rewards and the governmental machinery to secure physical development according to plan."

"According to plan" is a key phrase, and points to what may be a fundamental flaw in the new code as it has been developed to date. The Reporters address themselves to the question whether there are "any purposes of land-use regulation or any types of governmental development or control which should be made unavailable to a local government unless the community has a plan or unless the particular governmental decision is in acordance with a plan properly manifested?" The Reporters identify two "extreme" views on this crucial question. One is that a written plan for future land development, officially adopted by the local authority concerned, should control all governmental decisions concerning land development. The other extreme is that a local authority should be able to utilize all of its constitutional powers to control or influence development, whether it has a plan or not. The Reporters reject both these positions. They conclude that there are *some* powers and techniques of land-use control which can be exercised in a capricious or discriminatory form, and that the governing body should therefore not be able to use those powers "unless there is written evidence that forethought by the body was possible." The Reporters thus reach a conclusion which must give rise to very great misgivings. Their draft code requires an officially approved plan before a local government may make *certain* land development decisions. But "For most government decisions, such as a zoning ordinance, laying out the community into districts, no written plan is required prior to enactment of the local ordinance."

As this first draft of the new code is incomplete, it is not possible at this stage to trace in detail the way in which the Reporters intend to apply this distinction. One assumes that they proceed on the basis that so far as zoning and related powers of regulation are concerned, it should be possible, as well as highly desirable, to embody the principles on which the controls should be exercised, or the justification for the standards laid down, in the instrument of control itself. This reflects the concern of the lawyers, to which I referred in the concluding pages of my original report (see Part VI), to eliminate the scope for the arbitrary and discriminatory exercise of land-use controls by specifying, with as much certainty and precision as possible, the objects of control, the standards to be applied, and the circumstances in which they may be varied. These objectives, and the concern which underlies them, may well be justified in the political context of American local government, but it is absolutely no justification for concluding that a plan is unnecessary and can be dispensed with. It is no good building into the system of land-use controls an elaborate codification of principles and standards unless the exercise of these controls can be related to the wider context and objectives expressed in a comprehensive plan.

Planners should be alerted to what looks suspiciously like an attempt to comprehend the whole of the land-use planning process in the zoning ordinance itself, to the exclusion of the development (or "master") plan. Thus the conception and execution of land-use control becomes an exercise in legal draftsmanship and not a systematic application of the planning process—survey, analysis, plan, review. While the planning damsel in distress must welcome the providential arrival of the legal knight in shining armor (after some forty years' absence in the fleshpots of land-use litigation), it will hardly make for a happy ending if the result is the rape of the planning process rather than a felicitous marriage of planning skills and legal expertise.

The relationship between the zoning ordinance and the master plan has vexed American lawyers for many years. One recalls the entertaining dialogue invented by Charles

Haar[24] for the confusion of participants in his seminar on land-use controls at the Harvard Law School. The occasion is a hearing before a Committee on Planning and Zoning, in which the City Council is asked to overrule the action of the City Plan Commission which denied the request of an applicant to change the zoning of an unplatted tract of five acres from residential to light manufacturing:

A.: . . . . Mr. Beauvil, how do you conceive of the relationship of the zoning ordinance and your Master Plan?
B.: Zoning is the device by which those aspects of the Master Plan affecting private property are put into effect.
A.: The Zoning Map is the Land-Use Plan, then?
B.: No.
A.: You mean to say that the Zoning Map and the Land-Use Plan are different?
B.: Yes.
A.: How do they differ?

A tortuous argument ensues, but one feels that Mr. Beauvil, the Director of Planning for the City Plan Commission, puts up a creditable defense of the Master Plan when he concludes his case:

The Council recognized that the rapid growth of the city and the changing conditions therein might justify changes in the zoning ordinance in the future, and hence provided regulations and procedures for its amendment. With respect to the zoning ordinance, the Master Plan as it relates to land use is merely a complex guide for such changes. It is the antithesis of arbitrariness to set up objective standards for such changes, and that is all that the Land-Use Plan seeks to do.

The committee's decision is not recorded, and one would add that the Master Plan has wider functions than to act as a guide to legitimate zoning changes. Indeed, it is difficult to see how a zoning ordinance, involving as it does the

24. Charles M. Haar, *Land-Use Planning: A Casebook on the Use, Misuse, and Reuse of Urban Land* (Boston, Mass.: Little, Brown and Company, 1959), pp. 730–744.

regulation of land for specific uses, can be rationally constructed except on the basis of a comprehensive development plan. The zoning ordinance itself is not the development plan, but is one of the means by which the plan is implemented: it is a codification of land-use controls and development standards, whereas the development plan deals with the problems, needs, resources, policies, strategy, coordination, and programming of development and redevelopment.

To return to the Reporters and their Model Code, it is the more extraordinary that they should dismiss the need for a plan as the basis for control in that they provide in Article 2 an admirable specification for "land development plans," which defines in detail the purposes and preparation of the plan; the studies and surveys required; the statements of objectives, policies, and standards which it should contain; the programs by which the plan is to be implemented; and finally the process by which the plan is to be regularly reviewed, progress assessed, and policies revised.

The Reporters were evidently suffering from a degree of schizophrenia when they produced such an excellent blueprint for a development plan, and then proceeded to dismiss it as unnecessary in relation to "most governmental decisions" on land use and development. It is an unfortunate fact that whereas the 1922 Standard State Zoning Enabling Act was widely and enthusiastically adopted, the 1926 Standard City Planning Enabling Act remained pretty much a dead letter. One must fervently hope that the Reporters of the American Law Institute do not consign the land development plan section of their model code to the same fate.

It must be emphasized that this "Tentative Draft No. 1" of the Model Land Development Code represents work in progress and in no sense purports to be the finished product (several sections have not yet been drafted). But its scope, and the attempt which it represents to coordinate and rationalize the American system of land-use controls and development planning, can be briefly indicated by a summary of its present main structure.

The draft Code begins with the grant of power to control

or regulate future land development, and provides a much more limited (but very important) power to control existing land uses and buildings. It defines "development" as "any material change in the appearance of a parcel of land and its use or shape." This is the key definition since it delineates the scope of the power of a local government to control land under the Code, though one suspects that as a definition it will require a good deal further thought and refinement.[25]

The next section of the draft deals with the contents, preparation, and adoption of the land development plan, which I have discussed earlier. The essential point is that the plan itself confers no legal control over private or public landowners but is the policy statement to which certain powers of control and land acquisition are related.

The third section contains the primary powers of land-use control—zoning and subdivision. It incorporates many of the more modern techniques and provisions allowing for reasonable flexibility in their application. It also deals with the control of existing development or "nonconforming uses."

The fourth section provides a broad grant of power to local governments to acquire land by eminent domain (i.e., compulsorily) and to dispose of it to private developers in order "to secure development desired by the public authority." It also deals with the consequential problems of compensation and valuation. It is proposed that these generalized powers would replace all similar powers in existing law, urban redevelopment, and renewal statutes.

The next section is of great significance, in that it attempts to develop "a number of standards and principles where public authority cannot regulate the owner without compensation but, at the owner's request, must either pay him compensation or release his land from the regulation or control." This is designed to deal with certain types of case where regulation may be held to be an unconstitutional taking of private property. I discussed this aspect of American land-use control in Part VI, where I commented that

25. Compare the definition of "development" in the British Town and Country Planning Act 1962, Section 12.

The success of land-use controls in America probably owes everything to the fact that they have cost the taxpayer nothing. A crucial question facing American planners and their legal strategists is whether the urgent need to grapple with the problems of the exploding metropolis and the aging city can be met only by new measures of control accompanied by compensation for damage to property rights and values. That would be a complete break with the traditional basis of American land-use controls, and some are prepared to argue that it is one which the affluent society should be prepared to take in the interests of a better environment.

I also pointed, however, to the danger that any departure from the established convention—that land-use controls represent a legitimate exercise of the police power and therefore require no compensation—could rapidly lead to a demand that compensation should be paid for all types of land-use control; and that would almost certainly mean the end of effective land-use planning in America. My suggestion was that where the nature or degree of the control required was such as to be considered an unconstitutional use of the police power, it would be better to invoke the alternative power of eminent domain, and pay due compensation for the land or rights acquired, rather than attempt to graft compensation provisions onto the system of land-use controls exercised under the police power. This is a very delicate issue, which will require very careful handling if it is not to bring down the whole edifice of land-use control, without compensation, that has been built up over the past fifty years. One might also observe that if any general provision were introduced to compensate owners for adverse planning decisions, the corollary would arise of recouping for the public purse some part of the "betterment" realized by developers as a result of favorable decisions. Such provisions were introduced in the British Town and Country Planning Act 1947; they were repealed in 1952, but a similar charge was introduced again in the Land Commission Act 1967.

The next section of the draft Code deals with the enforcement of development controls, both by the traditional method of making a violation a legal "misdemeanor," and by administrative remedies such as a "cease and desist" order, injunctive procedures, and civil sanctions.

The draft Code then introduces another major innovation in establishing a state planning agency to adjudicate on disputes between neighboring local governments (e.g., where a regulation by one impinges on the welfare of the residents of an adjoining area) or where local regulations restrict or impede the location of regional facilities such as public utilities, interstate highways, etc. The state planning agencies would also be empowered to set aside a local regulation that it considered to be too restrictive; to review applications of local governments for federal assistance for development projects in order to determine whether the application best serves statewide interests; and itself to regulate land use in order to protect public facilities. This section thus reflects that body of opinion, to which I have referred earlier in this part, that envisages a much stronger role for the state government in planning matters than it has had in the past. I have also indicated that this wish to see the states play a larger and more effective part in land-use planning is by no means universal and may provoke much opposition. But it may well be at least as practical, probably much more so, as the alternative concept of new metropolitan planning agencies.

The next two sections deal with the appellate procedures: first the administrative review by the local agency, and then the judicial review by the courts. For the first, regular and standardized procedures are laid down, to introduce an element of order and consistency into what I described in Part V as the "usually farcical and always unsatisfactory" procedure for public hearings before Zoning Boards of Appeals. This is a very necessary improvement. As regards the process of judicial review, the Code introduces criteria for testing the validity of a local ordinance or decision. It is interesting to note that it is envisaged that the burden of sustaining the ordinance or decision would be greater where no land development plan has been adopted. The Reporters comment "Thus, one method of inducing local communities to plan will be to give more protection to an ordinance or administrative order of a community which has a plan." While welcoming this evidence that the Reporters see some merit in relating land-use controls to a plan, one must observe that it all depends on the quality of the plan.

The draft Code will also contain financial provisions to standardize the procedures for applying for federal or state grants-in-aid for local development, urban renewal, etc., and to authorize local governments to make grants to private developers "to secure private developments desired by the local government."

Finally, the draft Code envisages means of integrating decisions on land-use control into the public land record system.

The draft Code, even in its present tentative and unfinished state, is a most impressive and exciting achievement. It could, given the necessary support and momentum, represent by far the biggest advance in the American system of land-use control since Herbert Hoover issued the Standard State Zoning Enabling Act some forty-five years ago. But time is not on the side of the reformers. Herbert Wechsler, the Director of the American Law Institute, in a foreword to the draft Code, concluded "We recognize that the perfection and elaboration of the Model Act will be on our agenda for some years." With all due respect to the deliberativeness of legal thought, the need is urgent, and delay could damage the prospects of ever achieving what is now being attempted.

There is also a danger, however, that the resultant Model Land Development Code could be *too* perfect—so comprehensive and complete, so sophisticated in its conception and refined in its drafting that, if it were finally legislated and adopted, it could prove very difficult to amend and revise in the light of changing needs and developing techniques. Its authors must remember that land-use controls are part of the planning process, not the whole; and that, as those controls are generally expressed in legislative form, they can become a static element in what should be a dynamic process. This is a danger inherent in the statutory formulation of land-use controls, and it also reflects an approach to development planning which is likely to be increasingly invalid. Gordon Cherry, Deputy Director at the Centre for Urban and Regional Studies, University of Birmingham (England), recently gave expression to a different concept of planning, or of the problems with which the planner is involved:

A static outlook on planning has regarded the urban area as having a purely spatial physical form. The planner's job has been to conceive static distributions of land uses or activities. But a broader approach helps us to see the city not in these terms at all but as a complex interaction of interdependent units which are in a constant evolution and in a state of mutual adaptation. In this way the ecological structure suggests that the city is as much a social system in action as simply an artifact with a land-use pattern. The city is not just a spatial phenomenon; its features are cultural and not territorial in character.[26]

While one recognizes the validity of this approach, which regards the pattern of land use as the incidental reflection of a social system in action, this does not mean that the land-use pattern is irrelevant or that attempts to control land use are valueless. What it does mean is that the methods of control, and the way in which they are applied, must be related to social needs and economic realities and not merely to spatial phenomena.

The attraction of planning, both as an activity and as a subject for study, is that it cannot be static because it is dealing with a constantly changing situation and with continually changing public attitudes. The comparison of the American planning scene, in terms of land-use controls, as it appeared ten years ago and as it appears (at a distance) today is one illustration of this fascinating process.

26. *Surveyor—Local Government Technology,* Vol. CXXXIV, Number 3999 (24th January 1969), pp. 35–36.

APPENDIX

Extract from the Land Use Section of the Master Plan for San Francisco

A. *Objectives of the City-Wide Land Use Plan*

The City-Wide Land Use Plan of San Francisco is designed as a general guide to the attainment of the following objectives:

1. Improvement of the city as a place for living, by aiding in making it more healthful, safe, pleasant, and satisfying, with housing representing good standards for all families and by providing adequate open spaces and appropriate community facilities.

2. Improvement of the city as a place for commerce and industry by making it more efficient, orderly, and satisfactory for the production, exchange, and distribution of goods and services, with adequate space for each type of economic activity and improved facilities for the loading and movement of goods.

3. Organization of the two principal functional parts of the city—the working areas and the community areas—so that each may be clearly distinguished from but complementary to the other, and so that the economic, social, and cultural development of the city may be furthered.

4. Protection, preservation, and enhancement of the economic, social, cultural, and esthetic values that establish the desirable quality and unique character of the city.

5. Coordination of the varied pattern of land use with public and semipublic service facilities required for efficient functioning of the city, and for the convenience and well-being of its residents, workers, and visitors.

6. Coordination of the varied pattern of land use with cir-

146

culation routes and facilities required for the efficient movement of people and goods within the city, and to and from the city.

7. Coordination of the growth and development of the city with the growth and development of adjoining cities and counties and of the San Francisco Bay Region.

B. Principles of the City-Wide Land Use Plan

The City-Wide Land Use Plan is concerned with the city as a whole, and indicates generally how public and private land can be used best to promote the objectives of the plan.

The following principles are integral and basic elements of the City-Wide Land Use Plan:

1. The natural division of the city into two distinct functional areas—one primarily for production, distribution and services, and the other for residential purposes and the community facilities which are closely related to residential activities—should be recognized and encouraged.

2. The division of the two functional parts of the city into four working areas and twelve residential community areas should be recognized for planning purposes, with boundaries between such areas defined where practicable by traditionally accepted topographic or naturally formed limits or by the location of existing or proposed trafficways or open spaces.

3. A population holding capacity should be established for the city based on desirable and feasible density standards.

4. A population density pattern for the residential communities of the city should be established as a basis for determination of the location and extent of public and private facilities required to serve the community areas.

5. The pattern of desirable population densities should provide throughout the city opportunity for a wide range of building types to serve a variety of family sizes and income levels, without undue congestion in any one area.

6. The distribution of each category of population density as established in the standards of the City-Wide Land Use Plan should be guided by topographic and transportation considerations, as follows:

a. high density on easily accessible hilltops and ridges, along the edges of permanent open spaces and in closest proximity to public transit routes and major thoroughfares and to community business centers;
b. medium density on the slopes of hills and in proximity to public transit and secondary thoroughfares and to neighborhood shopping districts
c. low density on the most nearly level land and on land most distant from primary transportation routes.

7. Each of the community areas of the city should be defined and limited in extent to serve as an economic, social, and physical sub-unit of the city as a whole.

8. Within each residential community area the public and semi-public facilities, such as high school, junior high school, and playfield, should be grouped wherever possible into community centers easily accessible to all residents of the area.

9. The commercial facilities which serve all the residents of a community area should be assembled and compactly grouped into business centers convenient to but not directly on major trafficways and adjacent to the community centers.

10. Land for public and commercial facilities in each community area should be provided in equal proportion to the prospective population which will obtain under the standards of the City-Wide Land Use Plan.

11. The working areas of the city should be defined and designated in extent so as to increase the efficiency of each of the areas as a specialized center of management, production, or distribution.

12. The working areas of the city should be related to

the trafficways and transit systems so as to minimize time and distance in the journey to work from each of the community areas of the city and from within the San Francisco Bay Region.

Extract from San Francisco City Zoning Ordinance

Principal Uses Permitted, C-2 commercial district.

(a) Any principal use permitted in C-1 districts.

(b) Retail business or personal service establishment, not limited to sales or service, primarily for residents in the immediate vicinity, but not including any use first listed in a subsequent section of this Code.

(c) Printing shop, newspaper publication, blueprinting shop.

(d) Household repair shop, interior decorating shop, upholstering shop, sign painting shop, carpenter shop.

(e) Catering establishment.

(f) Theater, motel.

(g) Establishment for hand ironing only, not employing more than five (5) persons.

(h) Building contractor's office, including storage of incidental equipment and supplies entirely within the same building where provision is also made entirely within the structure for parking, loading and unloading of all vehicles used.

(i) Dry cleaning or dyeing shop, in connection with and incidental to a personal service establishment, but subject to all the limitations which are applied to an accessory use in Section 116 excepting the floor area limitation; and provided that no portion of a building occupied by such use shall have any ventilating flue, exhaust pipe or other opening, except fixed windows and exits required by law, within fifty (50) feet of any lot in any R residential district.

(j) Minor automobile repair shop, when conducted entirely within an enclosed building having no openings other than fixed windows or exits required by law within fifty (50) feet of any R residential district; not including any full body paint spraying or any body or fender repair except replacement, or any establishment where more than three (3) persons are regularly employed mechanics.

(k) Second-hand store.

(l) Amusement enterprise, including billiard hall, dance hall, night club, bowling alley, skating rink, shooting gallery, when conducted within a completely enclosed building; provided, (a) that incidental noise is reasonably confined to the premises by adequate soundproofing or other device, and (b) that no portion of a building occupied by such use shall have any opening, other than fixed windows and exits required by law, within fifty (50) feet of any lot in an R residential district.

(m) Amusement park, and related commercial amusement enterprises not conducted in completely enclosed buildings; provided, that the use lawfully existed at the effective date of this Code, or is so located that (a) the premises is not less than two hundred (200) feet from any R district, and (b) the aggregate area in the same or adjoining blocks occupied by existing amusement enterprises, is in excess of five (5) acres.

Extract from New York City Zoning Ordinance

Use Districts

Single-Family Detached Residence Districts

These districts are designed to provide a suitable open character for single-family detached dwellings at low densities. These districts also include community facilities and open uses which serve the residents of these districts or are benefited by an open residential environment.

General Residence Districts

These districts are designed to provide for all types of residential buildings in order to permit a broad range of housing types, with appropriate standards for each district on density, open space, and spacing of buildings. The various districts are mapped in relation to a desirable future residential density pattern, with emphasis upon accessibility to transportation facilities and to various community facilities, and upon the character of existing development. These districts also include community facilities and open uses which serve the residents of these districts or are benefited by an open residential environment.

Local Retail Districts

These districts are designed to provide for local shopping and include a wide range of retail stores and personal service establishments which cater to frequently recurring needs. Since these establishments are required in convenient locations near all residential areas, and since they are relatively unobjectionable to nearby residences, these districts are widely mapped. The district regulations are designed to promote convenient shopping and the stability of retail development by encouraging continuous retail frontage and

152

by prohibiting local service and manufacturing establishments which tend to breach such continuity.

Local Service Districts

These districts are designed to provide for a wide range of essential local services not involving regular local shopping. Since these establishments are less frequently visited by customers, they tend to break the continuity of prime retail frontage and, therefore, hamper the development of convenient shopping. The permitted services create relatively few objectionable influences for nearby residential areas.

Waterfront Recreation District

This district is designed to provide for the growing recreational activities of pleasure boating and fishing by permitting rental, servicing, and storage of boats in appropriate waterfront areas, normally adjacent to residential development.

General Commercial Districts

These districts comprise the City's major and secondary shopping centers, which provide for occasional family shopping needs and for essential services to business establishments over a wide area, and which have a substantial number of large stores generating considerable traffic. The district regulations are designed to promote convenient shopping and the stability of retail development by encouraging continuous retail frontage and by prohibiting service and manufacturing establishments which tend to break up such continuity.

Restricted Central Commercial Districts

These districts are designed to provide for office buildings and the great variety of large retail stores and related activities which occupy the prime retail frontage in the central business district, and which serve the entire metropolitan region. The district regulations also permit a few high-value custom manufacturing establishments which are generally associated with the predominant retail activities and which depend on personal contacts with persons living all over the region. The district regulations are also designed to provide for continuous retail frontage.

General Central Commercial Districts

These districts are designed to provide for the wide range of retail, office, amusement, service, custom manufacturing, and related uses normally found in the central business district, but to exclude non-retail uses which generate a large volume of trucking.

Commercial Amusement District

This district is designed to permit large open commercial amusement parks and is mapped in only a few areas.

General Service Districts

These districts are designed to furnish necessary services for a wider area than is served by the Local Service Districts. Since these service establishments often involve objectionable influences, such as noise from heavy service operations and large volumes of truck traffic, they are incompatible with both residential and retail uses. New residential development is excluded from these districts.

Light Manufacturing Districts (High Performance)

These districts are designed for a wide range of manufacturing and related uses which can conform to a high level of performance standards. Manufacturing establishments of this type, within completely enclosed buildings, provide a buffer between Residence (or Commercial) Districts and other industrial uses which involve more objectionable influences. New residential development is excluded from these districts, both to protect residences from an undesirable environment and to ensure the reservation of adequate areas for industrial development.

Medium Manufacturing Districts (Medium Performance)

These districts are designed for manufacturing and related activities which can meet a medium level of performance standards. Enclosure of such activities is not normally required except in areas along the boundary of a Residence District. No new residences or community facilities are permitted.

Heavy Manufacturing Districts (Low Performance)

These districts are designed to accommodate the essential heavy industrial uses which involve more objectionable influences and hazards, and which, therefore, cannot reasonably be expected to conform to those performance standards which are appropriate for most other types of industrial development. No new residences or community facilities are permitted.

Extract from New York City Zoning Ordinance[1]

Use Groups

Use Group 1
Single-family detached residential development

Use Group 2
Community facilities such as schools, libraries, or museums, which serve educational or other essential neighborhood needs or can function best in a residential environment, and are not objectionable in residential areas.

Use Group 4
Other community facilities, such as churches, community center, or hospitals, which provide recreational, health, or other essential services for residential areas or can function best in a residential environment, and are not objectionable in residential areas.

Use Group 5
Transient hotels. Permitted in all Commercial Districts, except C₃, but not in Residence or Manufacturing Districts.

Use Group 6
Retail and service establishments, such as food and small clothing stores, beauty parlors, dry cleaners, etc., which are needed to serve local shopping needs.

Use Group 7
Home maintenance and repair services like plumbing and electrical shops which are needed to serve nearby residential areas. These uses would be incompatible in prime retail shopping areas, because they interrupt the continuity of retail frontage.

Use Group 8
Amusement establishments such as small bowling alleys, and service uses such as upholstery and appliance repair shops, which appropriately serve nearby residential areas.

1. This is a somewhat simplified version of the full text.

Also suitable in secondary and major centers. They are not appropriate in local shopping areas or in the highly restricted central commercial areas.

Use Group 9
Services to business establishments and other services which depend on trade from a large area. They are therefore appropriately located in secondary, major, and central commercial areas and their peripheral service areas.

Use Group 10
Large retail establishments, such as department stores, which serve a large area. Appropriate in secondary, major and central shopping areas, but not in local shopping or local service areas because of the harmful effects of a large volume of traffic attracted from outside the neighborhood.

Use Group 11
Custom manufacturing activities, such as art needlework and jewelry manufacturing from precious metals, which have no significant objectionable effects and generate very little truck traffic. These establishments can best serve their customers from a central location, and are therefore appropriate in the central commercial areas.

Use Group 12
Large entertainment facilities, such as arenas and indoor skating rinks, which draw large numbers of people from a wide service area and generate high traffic volumes. Appropriate in secondary, major and general central commercial areas but not in local commercial areas nor in the restricted central commercial areas.

Use Group 13
Low coverage or open uses such as golf driving ranges, children's small amusement parks, and gasoline service stations. These are all uses which attract customers for special purposes not associated with retail shopping.

Use Group 14
Facilities for boating and related activities which are suitable in waterfront recreation areas.

Use Group 15
Large commercial amusement establishments, including the typical Coney Island attractions. They generate considerable noise and traffic and are appropriate only in a few designated areas like Coney Island or the Rockaways.

Use Group 16
Semi-industrial uses, including automotive and other services, such as custom welding shops, etc., which typically involve offensive noise and other objectionable influences. They are required to serve residential and commercial areas throughout the city, but are not compatible with residential uses or with other types of commercial development.

Use Group 17
Manufacturing uses which can normally conform to high performance standards by controlling objectionable influences and in so doing make them compatible to adjacent residential areas.

Use Group 18
Industrial uses which involve considerable danger of fire, explosion, or other hazards, or cannot be designed without appreciable expense to conform to high performance standards with respect to the emission of objectionable influences.

Extract from New York City Zoning Ordinance

Use Groups Permitted in Use Districts

USE GROUPS

DISTRICTS	Residential		Community Facilities		Retail and Commercial							Recreation				Gen. Ser.	Mfg.	
	1	2	3	4	5	6	7	8	9	10	11	12	13	14	15	16	17	18
Single-Family Detached Homes	□		□															
General Residence	□	□	□	□														
Local Retail	□	□	□	□	□	□												
Local Service	□	□	□	□	□	□	□											
Waterfront Recreation	□	□	□	□	□	□	□	□					□					
General Commercial	□	□	□	□	□	□	□	□	□	□		□						
Restricted Central Commercial	□	□	□	□	□	□	□	□	□	□	□							
Commercial Amusement	□	□	□	□	□	□	□	□	□	□	□	□	□	□	□			
General Service	□	□	□	□	□	□	□	□	□	□	□	□	□	□	□	□		
Light Manufacturing			□		□	□	□	□	□	□	□	□	□	□	□	□	□	
Medium Manufacturing						□	□	□	□	□	□	□	□	□	□	□	□	
Heavy Manufacturing						□	□	□	□	□	□	□	□	□	□	□	□	□

159

Extract from New York City Zoning Ordinance

Performance Standards Regulating Noise

Definitions

For the purpose of this Section, the following terms are defined:

Decibel
A "decibel" is a unit of measurement of the intensity of sound (the sound of pressure level).

Sound level meter
A "sound level meter" is an instrument standardized by the American Standards Association, which is used for measurement of the intensity of sound and is calibrated in decibels.

Octave band
An "octave band" is one of a series of eight bands which cover the normal range of frequencies included in sound measurements. Such octave bands serve to define the sound in terms of its pitch components.

Octave band analyzer
An "octave band analyzer" is an instrument used in conjunction with a sound level meter to measure sound in each of eight octave bands.

Impact noise filter
An "impact noise filter" is an instrument used in conjunction with the sound level meter to measure the peak intensities of short duration sounds.

Method of measurement

For the purpose of measuring the intensity or frequency of sound, the sound level meter, the octave band analyzer, and the impact noise filter shall be employed. The "flat" network and the "slow" meter response of the sound level meter shall be used. Sounds of short duration, as from forge hammers, punch presses, and metal shears, which cannot be measured accurately with the sound level meter, shall be measured with the impact noise filter as manufactured by the General Radio Company, or its equivalent, in order to determine the peak value of the impact. For sounds so measured, the sound pressure levels set forth in Section 42-213 (Maximum permitted decibel levels) may be increased by six decibels.

Maximum permitted decibel levels

In all Manufacturing Districts, the sound pressure level resulting from any activity, whether open or enclosed, shall not exceed at any point on or beyond any lot line, the maximum permitted decibel levels for the designated octave band as set forth in the following table for the district indicated.

In the enforcement of this regulation, sounds produced by the operation of motor vehicles or other transportation facilities shall not be included in determining the maximum permitted decibel levels.

Maximum Permitted Sound Pressure Levels (in decibels)

| Octave band | District | | |
(cycles per second)	M1	M2	M3
0 to 5	79	79	80
75 to 150	74	74	75
150 to 300	66	68	70
300 to 600	59	62	64
600 to 1200	53	56	58
1200 to 2400	47	51	53
2400 to 4800	41	47	49
above 4800	39	44	46

Special provisions applying along district boundaries

Whenever a Manufacturing District adjoins a Residence District, at any point at the district boundary or within the

Residence District, the maximum permitted decibel levels in all octave bands shall be reduced by six decibels from the maximum levels set forth in Section 42-213 (Maximum permitted decibel levels).

Extract from Santa Clara County Zoning Ordinance

Regulations for Professional Office Districts

1. Intent: A professional office district is created to accommodate a demonstrated need for the development of office space together with necessary landscaping and off-street parking facilities in locations served by primary access, yet inappropriate for commercial development because of close proximity to purely residential uses. It is intended that the professional office uses established in this district shall be designed and landscaped so as to be in harmony with such adjacent residential uses.

2. Uses Permitted: No building, structure or land shall be used and no building or structure shall hereafter be erected structurally, altered or enlarged except for the following uses:

a. *Residence:* All uses specified in the regulations for R-1, R-2, and R-3 Zoning Districts.

b. *Offices:* Subject in all cases to the issuance of an Architectural and Site Control Permit as specified in Section 34:

1. Administrative or Executive Offices: Similar to and including those pertaining to the management of office operations or the direction of enterprises but not including merchandising or sales services.

2. Professional Offices: Such as those pertaining to the practice of the professions and arts including but not limited to architecture, dentistry, engineering, law and medicine, but not including the sale of drugs or prescriptions except as incidental to the principal use and where there is no external evidence of such incidental use.

3. Research Laboratories: Such as those pertaining to investigation, analysis, or experimentation, to establish

163

new or revised findings and standards, subject in addition, in each case, to the securing of a use permit, as provided in Section 34.

3. *Development Standards:* The following minimum development standards are established as a guide to the issuance of an Architectural and Site Control Permit; subject, in each case, to the discretion of the Planning Commission as to such more restrictive requirements as may be appropriate in order to ensure harmony with adjacent uses of land:

a. *Height:* Two and one half stories but not to exceed thirty-five (35) feet.

b. *Lot Coverage:* Buildings within foundation lines not to exceed twenty-five percent (25%) of lot area.

c. *Yards:* Front yard twenty-five (25) feet, no portion of which may be used for required off-street parking; side and rear yards equal to those required in nearest adjacent residence zone.

d. *Off-Street Parking:* A number of stalls, at the discretion of the Planning Commission, such as to ensure complete off-street parking for both employees and clients.

e. *Landscaping:* Such as to ensure harmony with adjacent residential areas.

f. *Signs:* For identification only, to be located upon the face of the building, with no flashing or moving lights.

Extract from Oakland City Zoning Ordinance

Travel Accommodations Combining District

Purpose. The purpose of the "T" District shall be to provide sleeping accommodations and convenience facilities for travellers along state highways, other heavily travelled arterial routes, or adjacent to the central commercial district; and to minimize the impact of travel accommodations and convenience facilities on residential uses.

Districts Combined with "T" District. Certain Commercial and Residential Districts or portions thereof may be combined with the "T" District when so indicated on the Zoning District Map.

"T" District Regulations and Uses. In the "T" District the following regulations shall apply and the following uses only are permitted, in addition to those regulations and uses herein specified as applicable to and permitted in the respective district with which the "T" District has been combined.

1. Motels and hotels, together with dining rooms, news stands signs and other facilities incidental to a motel or hotel, excluding service stations, subject to the following conditions:

    (a) Structures and other improvements shall be built or installed in accord with a site plan approved by the City Planning Commission with respect to location of structures, layout and improvement of off-street parking and loading areas, location and width of driveways, ingress and egress to and from the site, and location and planting of landscaped areas, and location and design of lighting and signs.

    (b) Wherever the site adjoins a residential site, a suitable wall or fence not less than five (5) feet in height shall be erected, and whenever an area designated on the site plan for off-street parking or off-street loading adjoins a residential site, in addition to the wall or fence, and ad-

165

jacent thereto, a landscaped strip not less than four (4) feet in depth shall be planted and permanently maintained: or, in the alternative, wherever the site adjoins a residential site, a compact evergreen hedge not less than five (5) feet in height shall be planted and permanently maintained; provided that in a required front yard or within fifty feet of a street intersection the height of the wall, fence or hedge shall be limited to three and one-half (3½) feet.

(c) If the premises or signs are illuminated, lighting shall be deflected away from adjoining residential site so as to cause no annoying glare.

(d) Sufficient room for turning or maneuvering vehicles shall be provided on the site.

(e) Driveways and off-street parking and off-street loading areas shall be paved so as to provide a durable, dustless surface and shall be so graded and drained as to dispose of surface water without its draining on adjoining property.

(f) Bumper rails shall be provided where needed for safety or to protect property.

(g) Off-street parking spaces shall be provided for a dining room in the ratio of one parking space for each one hundred (100) square feet floor area, or fraction thereof, of such dining room or other rooms, interior patios or courts, designed and used for serving meals.

(h) There shall be off-street parking spaces in a ratio of not less than seventy-five per cent (75%), or nearest fraction thereof, of the total number of sleeping rooms provided.

2. Non-flashing, indirectly illuminated signs, subject to the following limitations:

(a) On the sign of a motel or hotel one (1) identification sign not exceeding forty (40) square feet in area, endorsement signs the total area of which shall not exceed fifteen (15) square feet and informative signs the total area of which shall not exceed ten (10) square feet.

(b) No signs shall extend over any property line.

(c) For the purpose of this section, an endorsement sign shall include a sign of any firm or association which endorses a motel or hotel as to the quality of its service or accommodations; and an informative sign shall include any of the following: "Office," "TV," "Quiet Please," "Entrance," "(No) Vacancy," or other information of a similar nature.

(d) Where the "T" district has been combined with a Residential District, no window sign or other display or sign shall be used to advertise such use except an inside window sign not to exceed two (2) square feet, flat against the window; which said sign may be electric or neon, but shall not be of a flashing type.

Extract from New York City Zoning Ordinance

Special Permits: Gasoline Service Stations

In any C_2 or C_6 Commercial District whose longer dimension is 375 feet or more (exclusive of land in streets), the Board may permit gasoline service stations, provided that the following findings are made:

(a) That such use will serve the needs of the surrounding local community, which otherwise would not be served adequately by gasoline service stations located within nearby districts where such use is permitted as of right.

(b) That the site for such use has a minimum area of 7500 square feet.

(c) That the site for any such use which is not located on an arterial highway or a major street has a maximum area of 15,000 square feet.

(d) That the vehicular entrances or exits shall not be located within an area of restricted access relating to entrances or exits intended for the use of children attending schools or playgrounds accessory thereto, or relating to entrances or exits to public parks or public playgrounds with an area of one-half acre or more.

The Board shall prescribe the following conditions:

(a) That any lubrication facilities are located within a completely enclosed building.

(b) That the site is so designed as to provide reservoir space for five waiting automobiles within the zoning lot in addition to spaces available within an enclosed lubritorium or at the pumps.

(c) That entrances and exits are so planned that at maximum expected operation, vehicular movement into or from the gasoline service station will cause a minimum of obstruction on streets or sidewalks.

(d) That the zoning lot is screened along any rear lot line or side lot line adjoining a Residence District by either:

    (1) A strip of at least four feet wide, densely planted with

168

shrubs or trees at least four feet high at the time of planting and which are of a type which may be expected to form a year-round dense screen at least six feet high within three years, or

(2) A wall or barrier or uniformly painted fence of fire-resistant material at least six feet high, but not more than eight feet above finished grade. Such wall, barrier or fence may be opaque or perforated, provided that not more than 50 percent of its face is open.

(e) The accessory business signs shall be subject to the applicable district sign regulations, provided that:

(1) A maximum of 11 square feet of signs customarily displayed on the sides of a pump shall not be included in computing the total surface area of the signs on the zoning lot.

(2) In C_2 Districts, the provision set forth in Section 32-622 (non-illuminated signs) limiting the area of illuminated, non-flashing signs to a maximum of 50 square feet shall not apply, provided that the total area of all illuminated, non-flashing, or non-illuminated signs on a zoning lot shall not exceed 150 square feet.

That Board may prescribe additional appropriate conditions and safeguards to minimize adverse effects on the character of the surrounding area, and to protect residential zoning lots which are adjoining or across the street.

Extract from Proposed Controls for Terrace Housing: El Paso, Texas (1960)

"Floating Zone"

Standards for R.6. Zone: single-family attached dwellings

A. The tract shall include a minimum usable area of 3 acres.

B. There should be a maximum of 25 dwelling units per acre.

C. There should be a minimum of one off-street parking space per dwelling unit.

D. The minimum lot width should be not less than 18 (20) feet.

E. The minimum corner lot width should be not less than 28 (30) feet.

F. There should be a lot depth of not less than 90 feet.

G. There should be a lot area of not less than 1620 square feet.

H. At least 60 per cent of the net lot area should be open space.

I. The maximum height of structures should be two stories.

J. All sites should have frontage on a dedicated public way, with a minimum width of 40 feet.

K. There should be no detached accessory structures permitted. All accessory uses should be included as part of the main dwelling and conforming to the space requirements for that building.

L. The number of dwelling units per structure should not exceed eight (144 feet maximum length).

M. The pattern of parking for each structure of eight units or less should be the same except for corner units. Parking for these units, if required to protect vision clearance at the street intersection, may be located at the front of the building.

N. Consideration should be given to providing all parking areas next to the street, while locating all pedestrian activities at the rear of the lot.

Extract from San Francisco City Zoning Ordinance

Planned Unit Development

The authorization of a Planned Unit Development as described herein, shall be subject to the following additional conditions. The Planning Commission may authorize the development as submitted or may modify, alter, adjust or amend the plan before authorization, and in authorizing it may prescribe other conditions as provided in this Code. The development as authorized shall be subject to all conditions so imposed, and shall be excepted from other provisions of this Code only to the extent specified in the authorization.

1. The application must be accompanied by an over-all development plan showing the use or uses, dimensions and locations of proposed structures, of parking spaces, and of areas, if any, to be reserved for streets, parks, playgrounds, school sites and other open spaces, with such other pertinent information as may be necessary to a determination that the contemplated arrangement or use makes it desirable to apply regulations and requirements differing from those ordinarily applicable under this Code.

2. The tract or parcel of land involved must be either in one ownership or the subject of an application filed jointly by the owners of all the property included or by the Redevelopment Agency of the City. It must constitute all or part of a Redevelopment Project Area, or if not must either include an area of at least three (3) acres or be bounded on all sides by streets, public open spaces or the boundary lines of less restrictive use districts.

3. The proposed development must be designed to produce an environment of stable and desirable character, and must provide standards of open space and permanently reserved areas for off-street parking adequate for the occupancy

172

proposed, and at least equivalent to those required by the terms of this Code for such occupancy in the zoning district. It must include provision for recreation areas to meet the needs of the anticipated population or as specified in the Master Plan.

A conditional use of this category may contain, as an integral part of a residential development, a shopping center for service to the residents, if designed as a unit of limited size and controlled by more restrictive and specific regulations than would result from a reclassification of the area so used to a Commercial District. No other commercial use of any Planned Unit Development in any Residential district shall be authorized except an office building or buildings to be occupied primarily by administrative, clerical, accounting or business research organizations, where the principal use does not involve any of the following:

1. The handling or display on the premises of any merchandising services except as permitted as an accessory use for the accommodation of the occupants;

2. Frequent personal visits of clients, members or customers or other persons not employed on the premises;

3. Show windows or exterior display advertising of any kind.

Extract from Oakland City Zoning Ordinance

Regulations for Medical Center District

SEC. 7-1. 4880 Purpose. The purpose of the "S. I." Medical Center District is to promote the general welfare of the citizens of Oakland by encouraging adequate health services to the community, through the enhancement of the amenity and effective operation of centers of medical activities in the City, through the protection of patterns of development that may be served efficiently by public facilities.

SEC. 7-1. 4881 Permitted Use Regulation. Subject to the provisions of this Section, the following uses only are permitted in the "S-1" District:

> (a) Medical uses including general hospitals, convalescent hospitals, doctors' and dentists' offices and clinics, medical diagnostic and research laboratories, and similar medical facilities utilized in the investigation, diagnosis, treatment, and care of physical and psychological illnesses and injuries of human beings.
>
> (b) Multiple dwellings and group dwellings according to the following standard; for each dwelling unit in the "S-1" District there shall be a lot area of not less than two hundred (200) square feet; provided that if the total lot area divided by two hundred (200) leaves a remainder of less than two hundred (200) square feet but of one hundred (100) square feet or more, one (1) additional dwelling unit may be constructed.
>
> (c) Structures designed to provide group living accommodations only.
>
> (d) Off-street parking and loading facilities provided such facilities shall be subject to the regulations of Section 7-1. 4885 hereof.
>
> (e) Accessory buildings customarily incident to any permitted or conditional use upon the same lot; provided, that no such building shall be

located in any required front yard or side yard. (f) A sign identifying a permitted or conditional use located on the site; and a sign not exceeding six (6) square feet in area, appertaining only to the lease, hire, sale or display of a building or premise.

SEC. 7-1. 4882 Conditional Uses. Subject to the provisions of this Section, the following uses only may be permitted in the "S-1" District upon the granting of a use permit in this Article; provided that these conditional uses may be located only within a structure principally occupied by a permitted use pursuant to Section 7-1. 4881 hereof:

(a) Service establishments and professional offices which have the medical center as their principal service area and which supply retail goods or offer services of a professional, medical or personal nature to permitted uses or to the patients, practitioners, or employees thereof.

SEC. 7-1. 4883 Action of the City Planning Commission Relating to Conditional Use Permit. The City Planning Commission, after a public hearing held in accordance with the provisions of this Article, may grant or deny a Use Permit, and in granting a Use Permit may attach such conditions as the facts warrant. On the basis of the application and the evidence submitted, the Planning Commission shall by resolution make the following findings prior to issuing a Use Permit:

(a) That the establishment serves primarily the medical center in which it is located, and that in size, arrangement, and location it is incidental to the primary medical function of the area.

(b) That adequate off-street parking is to be provided and that the operation of the proposed service will not cause undesirable traffic congestion nor attract an objectionable volume of additional traffic into the "S-1" District.

Extract from Santa Clara County Zoning Ordinance

Regulations for Restricted Agricultural Districts

Sec. 44.1 The following regulations shall apply in any "A" —Restricted Agricultural District:

Sec. 44.2 Uses Permitted: No building structure or land shall be used and no building or structure shall be hereafter erected, structurally altered or enlarged except for the following uses:

Nurseries	Botanical Conservatory
Greenhouses	Field and Truck crops
Arboreta	Orchards and Vineyards
Forest Land	Landscape Gardening
Drying of Crops	Storage, bottling and
Animal Breeding	wholesaling of wine
Apiary	Riding Academies and
	Stables
Fur Farm	Dairies & Processing
	Dairy Products
Guest Ranch	Poultry Raising, Eggs
	& Hatcheries
Pasture	Hay & Straw Sale and
	Storage

Live Stock Ranches

Sec. 44.3 Subject to the above provisions, uses customarily incident to any of the listed permitted uses may be maintained and specifically the following:

Sec. 44.3.1 Residence of the owner or owners or leasee or lessor of the land upon which the use is conducted.

Sec. 44.3.2 Residence of other members of the family of those mentioned in Section 44.3.1.

Sec. 44.3.3 Residence of bona fide employees of those mentioned in Section 44.3.1 and 44.3.2.

Sec. 44.4 Conditional uses: The following conditional uses

may be established in an "A"—Restricted Agricultural District subject to the securing of a Use Permit as provided in Section 35 of this Ordinance:

SCHOOL (elementary and high) and

CHURCH (except rescue mission or temporary revival);

PARK, PLAYGROUND OR COMMUNITY CENTER, owned and operated by governmental agency or a non-profit community organization; and

GOLF COURSE (except driving tee or range, miniature course and similar uses operated for commercial purposes);

PERMANENT FARM LABOR CAMP

A Statement of Policy by the Santa Clara County Planning Commission

Exclusive Agricultural Zoning

Purpose   Agricultural zoning is intended to protect prime agricultural soil and valid agricultural enterprises. It is intended to be applied in accordance with a master plan of land use based on soil quality and other factors pertinent to the conservation of agriculture.

Its effect is to restrict and control the infiltration of urban development into areas generally devoted to agriculture so that the continuance of this activity may be assured for the foreseeable future.

Policy   1. The extension of agricultural zones shall generally be upon the request of property owners who are engaged in valid agricultural operations and in accordance with a master plan of land use.

2. Failure to protest such zoning at the time of public hearing shall be deemed to constitute consent of the property owners involved.

3. All applications and petitions filed for such zoning will receive careful detailed consideration and study with respect to established criteria in order to determine whether the area qualifies as an exclusive agricultural zone.

This shall be accomplished by the technical staff of the Commission by offices review, field inspection, and public hearing.

4. The establishment of exclusive agriculture zoning shall be designed in general to create large contiguous blocks of agricultural land, either by original petition or by the annexation of smaller holdings to existing blocks.

5. It is not the intention to zone land which is not

predominantly used for agriculture as exclusive agriculture.

6. It is not the intention to use the exclusive agricultural zone to thwart the reasonable aspirations of cities for orderly growth.

Extract from the Code of the City of New Orleans Vieux Carré Commission (1958)

Compulsory Maintenance of Historic Buildings

Preservation of structures in the Vieux Carré by the owner or other person having legal custody thereof. All buildings and structures in that section of the City of New Orleans known as the Vieux Carré section . . . shall be preserved against decay and deterioration, and free from certain structural defects in the following manner, by the owner thereof, or such other person who may have the legal custody and control thereof. The said owner or other person having legal custody and control thereof shall repair said building if it be found to have any of the following defects:

A. Those which have parts thereof which are so attached that they may fall and injure members of the public or property.

B. Deteriorated or inadequate foundation.

C. Defective or deteriorated flooring or floor supports, or flooring or floor supports of insufficient size to carry imposed loads with safety.

D. Members of walls, partitions or other vertical support that split, lean, list or buckle due to defective material or deterioration.

E. Members of walls, partitions or other vertical supports that are insufficient size to carry imposed loads with safety.

F. Members of ceilings, roofs, ceiling and roof supports, or other horizontal members which sag, split, or buckle due to defective material or deterioration.

G. Members of ceilings, roofs, ceiling and roof supports, or other horizontal members that are of sufficient size to carry imposed loads with safety.

180

H. Fireplaces or chimneys which list, bulge, or settle, due to defective material or deterioration.

I. Fireplaces or chimneys which are of insufficient size or strength to carry imposed loads with safety.

J. Deteriorated or ineffective waterproofing of exterior walls, roofs, foundations, or floors, including broken windows or doors.

K. Defective or lack of weather protection for exterior wall coverings, including lack of paint, or weathering due to lack of paint or other protective covering.

L. Any fault or defect in the building which renders the same structurally unsafe or not properly watertight.

Duty of Vieux Carré Commission to Assist in Enforcement of this Article: It shall be the duty of the Vieux Carré Commission through its Director, or other proper officer, to send notices to all persons who may be guilty of a violation of this Article and inform them of defects in their buildings or structures which must be remedied, in compliance with this ordinance. If such notice has not been complied with after 30 days shall elapse from the giving of such notice, then it shall be the duty of the Director of the Vieux Carré Commission to prosecute, or to cause to have prosecuted, such violations of this Article in the Municipal Courts of the City of New Orleans, or such other court of competent jurisdiction as may be proper, either civil or criminal. This duty shall not be mandatory where said Director believes, or has good reason to believe that the person to whom notice has been sent is complying, or attempting to comply with the provisions of this Article.

Extract from Chicago City Zoning Ordinance

Standards for Variations

The Board of Appeals shall not vary the regulations of this comprehensive amendment, as authorized in this Ordinance unless it shall make findings based upon the evidence presented to it in each specific case that:

A. The property in question cannot yield a reasonable return if permitted to be used only under the conditions allowed by the regulations in the district in which it is located;

B. The plight of the owner is due to unique circumstances; and

C. The variation, if granted, will not alter the essential character of the locality.

For the purpose of implementing the above rules, the Board shall also, in making its determination whether there are practical difficulties or particular hardships, take into consideration the extent to which the following facts favorable to the applicant have been established by the evidence.

1. The particular physical surroundings, shape, or topographical condition of the specific property involved would result in a particular hardship upon the owner as distinguished from a mere inconvenience, if the strict letter of the regulations were carried out;

2. The conditions upon which the petition for a variation is based would not be applicable, generally, to other property within the same zoning classification;

3. The purpose of the variation is not based exclusively upon a desire to make more money out of the property;

4. The alleged difficulty or hardship has not been created by any person presently having an interest in the property.

5. The granting of the variation will not be detrimental to

the public welfare or injurious to other property or improvements in the neighborhood in which the property is located; and

6. The proposed variation will not impair an adequate supply of light and air to adjacent property, or substantially increase the danger of fire, or endanger the public safety, or substantially diminish or impair property values within the neighborhood.

The Board of Appeals may impose such conditions and restrictions upon the premises benefited by a variation as may be necessary to comply with the standards set out in this Section to reduce or minimize the injurious effect of such variation upon other property in the neighborhood, and better to carry out the general intent of this comprehensive amendment.

Extract from Proposed Sub-Division Regulations Phoenix, Arizona (1960)

Development Master Plan

A Development Master Plan shall be prepared prior to preparation and submission of the initial Preliminary Plat *whenever*, in the opinion of the Department, the tract is sufficiently large to comprise an entire neighborhood, or the tract initially proposed for platting is only a portion of a larger land-holding of the Subdivider, or, the tract is a part of a larger land area the development of which is complicated by unusual topographic, utility, land use, land ownership or other conditions. The entire land area need not in this case be under the subdivider's control.

a. *Preparation*: The Development Master Plan shall be prepared to a scale and accuracy commensurate with its purpose, and shall include:
1. General street pattern with particular attention to collector streets and future circulation throughout the neighborhood.
2. General location and size of school sites, parks or other public areas.
3. Location of shopping centers, multi-family residential or other proposed land uses.
4. Methods proposed for sewage disposal water supply and storm drainage.

b. *Submission and Review:* The subdivider shall submit five (5) copies of the DMP to the Department for its review for compliance with public objectives giving special attention to the following:
1. Street and thoroughfares as related to neighborhood circulation and the City Streets and Highways Plan.
2. Sewerage, water supply, drainage or flood control methods or systems as related to the existing or planned public systems.
3. Location of any proposed commercial development as

184

related to existing or anticipated community or neighborhood need.

4. Land required for schools, parks or other public use; the general amount and location of public land; the approximate timing of acquisition shall be tentatively determined at this stage. Copies of the DMP shall be transmitted by the Department to such other offices whose review is deemed necessary to sound planning.

Extract from Proposed Sub-Division Regulations Phoenix, Arizona (1960)

Programming by Indirection

Sanitary Sewage Disposal: Sewage disposal facilities shall be installed to serve each lot and be subject to the following standards and approvals:

a. Individual systems may be constructed only in areas not reasonably accessible to a public sewer system, and then only when the following conditions are met to the satisfaction of the County Health Department:

   1. Soil absorptivity is adequate.

   2. Construction complies with approved standards.

   3. Location of septic tank and seepage pits or leach lines or disposal beds in relation to property lines, and water supply wells and lines are acceptable. Location shall be such that efficient and economical connection can be made to a future public sewer.

b. Public sanitary sewer shall be installed in areas which are reasonably accessible to an existing sewer system and shall be constructed to plans, profiles and specifications approved by the City Water and Sewer Department and the City Engineer. Where existing sewers are inadequate to serve the new subdivision, the Subdivider may be required to connect with sewers capable of carrying the additional load. Where further development beyond the limits of the proposed subdivision appears probable, the Subdivider may be required to install larger mains to handle additional development.

c. In areas where public sanitary sewer is not reasonably accessible but where plans for a public system have been prepared and approved, and construction is programmed within a period of 5 years, the Subdivider shall plan and construct sewers within and for the subdivision for connection with such planned public system even though such connection is not immediately possible. In such cases, the Subdivider shall provide for interim sewage disposal by a method approved by the County Health Department.

Water Supply: Each lot shall be supplied with safe, pure and potable water in sufficient volume and pressure for domestic use and fire protection, subject to the following standards.

a. Individual wells may be installed where it can be shown that future development will be scattered or lots so few as to render a public water system unfeasible, provided that the following conditions are met to the satisfaction of the County Health Department:

1. Supply is adequate in quantity and quality.

2. Well is located not closer than 100 feet to any septic tank, seepage pit or leach line, whether located on subject lot or on another.

b. Wherever economically feasible or wherever individual systems cannot meet County Health Department requirements, a community water system shall be planned and constructed to approved City standards. Water plans shall be accompanied by a letter from the owning agency or corporation insuring that adequate water service will be supplied and maintained commencing with the occupancy of the first lot developed.

Extract from the New Haven–Church Street Redevelopment Plan

Redevelopment Standards

Controls, Regulations and Standards for Development of Real Property

A. *Blocks A, B, C, and D*

1. These blocks are to be developed as a unified central city commercial-retail center. While the redeveloper will be given freedom in concept, design and layout within the standards herein specified, there are certain criteria upon which these standards are based and upon which the proposals of the redeveloper will be judged.

The redeveloper will be required to obtain the approval of the Redevelopment Agency which shall request the written opinion of the City Plan Commission on all proposals. In addition to conformance to the standards contained herein, the proposals of the redeveloper will be evaluated as to the manner in which the proposal achieves the objectives of the plan.

This review of the proposal will be made in accordance with the following criteria:

(a) The proposed uses shall be distributed over the area of the four blocks in a manner to create optimum reuse and shall not be concentrated within a portion of the total area.

(b) The various frontages shall be developed with continuous related uses in order to produce the greatest impact as an integrated unit.

(c) The proposed uses shall be developed to create a center which will be commercially attractive and a focal point of social interest for the community as a whole.

(d) The various elements of the plan shall be connected by an internal pedestrian circulation system designed as an integral part of the development, so as to create for the pedestrian comfort and ease of movement within the proposed structures.

(e) The services (i.e. parking and trucking) to the proposed uses must be integrated with pedestrian and vehicular patterns, as may be the case, both inside and outside the development area.

(f) The concept and design must reflect the most advanced architectural concepts and technique so as to provide lasting interest and strength.

In order to assist in obtaining the objectives of the above criteria there will be no retained utility easements in the area of the four blocks. Gregson Alley and Center Street will be closed, and the redeveloper may, at his option, accept the subsurface and air rights over George Street and Crown Street, with the City retaining surface rights to those streets.

2. The following uses will be required. The distribution, intensity and introduction of additional uses shall be subject to the approval of the Redevelopment Agency which shall request the written opinion of the City Plan Commission on all proposals.

(a) Retail uses of the type ordinarily found in central city shopping areas. Examples of these are general merchandise, apparel, furniture and home furnishings, drugs, books, florist and personal service shops, etc., not less than 450,000 square feet—Maximum of 700,000 square feet.

(b) Commercial uses to include professional offices, offices, office space and banking space.—Maximum of 275,000 square feet.

(c) A commercial hotel to include a lounge, dining rooms, banquet facilities and ballroom.

3. Off Street Loading. All loading berths must be off street and must not overlap any traffic lanes. Surface level berths may be located only off George Street, Temple Street and the north frontage road of the Oak Street Connector. No curb cuts may be within 25 feet of any street intersection.

The number of loading berths shall be subject to the following standards:

(a) For each retail store—1 berth or if the redeveloper can demonstrate to the satisfaction of the Redevelopment Agency that a group of stores can operate efficiently from centralized loading facilities then in the case of stores each under 10,000 square feet in gross floor area one berth for an aggregate of 40,000 square feet of gross floor area for each such group of stores, provided, however, that a minimum of one loading berth shall be provided for each 40,000 square feet of gross floor area, or fraction thereof.

(b) For hotel, office buildings, and other commercial uses —1 loading berth for each 60,000 square feet of gross floor area or fraction thereof.

(c) The redeveloper must demonstrate that the size of loading berths is adequate to meet the operational requirements of the uses proposed. In lieu of such a demonstration the size required shall be at least 10 feet wide, 14 feet high and 45 feet deep, exclusive of access aisles and maneuvering space.

4. Parking. Parking facilities will be provided by the Parking Authority of the City of New Haven in an amount equal to 25% of the gross floor area of the total development, above and below grade. The redeveloper shall coordinate his plans with those of the Parking Authority in order to encourage pedestrian movements from the parking areas to the commercial-retail center.

5. Setbacks, Towers, Coverage. Ground floor coverage may exceed 80% of the total area only if the proposal provides for development of roof terraces available to the public for use, such as a restaurant, to an extent and in manner deemed suitable to the Redevelopment Agency which shall obtain the written opinion of the City Plan Commission thereon. The objective of this requirement is to insure the achievement of an openness and attractiveness of the overall project. The height of any structures to be built on a street or property line shall not exceed 70 feet, provided, however,

that a tower may extend above this height if the portion to be so extended is set back 20 feet from the street lines of Church, Chapel and Temple Streets and the north frontage road of the Oak Street Connector.

6. The redeveloper may construct at the second story level over the Church Street sidewalk a one-story pedestrian concourse in order to encourage pedestrian traffic to possible second-story shops. It shall be the responsibility of the redeveloper to provide and maintain necessary lighting facilities for the area of the Church Street sidewalk under this projection.

7. Signs. Flashing illuminated exposed neon signs and signs other than those relating to business on the site shall not be permitted. Non-illuminated signs may be belt type or perpendicular.

Illuminated non-flashing signs must be belt type signs. The gross area of signs allotted to each store or individual use for each street façade shall not exceed 100 square feet or 10% of the ground floor level on which the store or use is located nor may it project more than 24 inches from the face of the building. No signs will be permitted on awnings, marquees or the projection over the Church Street sidewalk. To assure uniform development the redeveloper shall submit the sign designs to the Redevelopment Agency for its approval. The Redevelopment Agency shall request the written opinion of the City Plan Commission prior to approving any proposed standards.

Extract from the Washington, D. C., Columbia Plaza Urban Renewal Plan

Design Objectives

a. To create a functionally and visually unified development through architectural treatment and the creation of a Plaza Area.

b. To maximize in both architectural design and in site planning the environmental factors, such as existing and proposed streets, changes in grade, architectural elements and adjacent Federal and institutional establishments.

c. To maintain and improve existing vistas and visual axis from, on or about the Urban Renewal Area particularly with respect to the following:

1. The view of Washington Monument along Virginia Avenue;
2. The view of the Lincoln Memorial along 23rd Street;
3. The proposed E Street Mall; and
4. The proposed National Cultural Center on the banks of the Potomac River.

d. To develop to the maximum extent possible the potential of this site in regard to the overlook that it will have of the National Cultural Center and the Potomac River and, at the same time, to secure an appropriate and a significant architectural treatment of all buildings to be constructed within the Urban Renewal Area so as to take maximum advantage of the vista of this site from the National Cultural Center, the Inner Loop Freeway, the Potomac and George Washington Memorial Parkways, etc.

e. To develop the 23rd Street frontage as the primary pedestrian access to the area.

f. To provide both vehicular and pedestrian access to the Project from Virginia Avenue and 23rd Street, since the other two sides are adjacent to expressways. Such vehicular and pedestrian access should be coordinated with existing and proposed developments in the Area.

g. To provide pedestrian access to the National Cultural Center and to the Naval Observatory Hill which are to be coordinated with open-space development within the Area.

h. To provide two types of open space within the Plaza Area:

1. Primarily for the use of residents of the area (providing maximum privacy in conjunction with sitting and recreation areas, a swimming pool and appropriate landscaping): and

2. For joint use by residents of the Area and the public at large.

Extract from Chairman's Brief for Architectural Advisory Panel on developers' proposals for Golden Gateway Redevelopment San Francisco

Basic Questions

A. *Architectural*

1. Will the project be an example of distinguished civic design and architecture?
2. Will it contribute to the delight and well-being of the citizens of the city?
3. Has proper consideration been given to scale?
4. Should the project reflect the traditions of the city and provide for continuity between old and new?

B. *Social*

1. Does the project provide a delightful environment for its inhabitants?
2. Will it contribute to the environment of bordering areas?
3. Have local climatic factors been considered?
4. Have appropriate facilities been provided for community use?
5. How does the proposal's treatment of population density, percentage of land covered, type of housing and commercial units affect the lives of the inhabitants?
6. What are the implications to the city in regard to public health and law enforcement?

C. *Economic*

(Note: This Panel is not primarily concerned with financial evaluations but its comments in this field are welcome.)
1. Is the direct cost of the project within reason?
2. Will continuous maintenance costs be low enough that the area can be kept in good condition?

194

3. Will indirect costs to the city for all services be reasonable?

4. Are the ranges of residential units by size and the commercial spaces suitable for the potential market?

D. *Future Growth*

1. Does the proposed design enhance the possibility of redevelopment or new construction in adjacent areas?

E. *Existing Features*

1. Does the proposal provide a harmonious relationship with such features as Customs House, Jackson Square, Telegraph Hill, Portsmouth Square, and the future Ferry Park and Harbor developments?

F. *Effect on the City*

1. What will be the impact of the proposed development on existing and planned streets, freeways, utilities and other city services?

2. How does the proposal relate to existing regulations and codes?

3. If the proposal were accepted, would there be any special financial impacts on the city?

G. *Circulation*

1. Does the proposal relate itself to the existing freeway plan? to existing and proposed public transportation facilities?

2. How well does the proposal treat parking and general access of all vehicular transportation to the area?

3. Has the pedestrian received proper consideration in terms of isolating and protecting him from all types of vehicular traffic?

4. Can the city adopt the circulation concept proposed and expand it to the surrounding areas without great difficulty?

5. Has vertical circulation been properly solved within the structures proposed?

H. *Landscaping*

1. Are appropriate landscaped areas provided such as parks, park-strips, malls, gardens, courts, and playgrounds?
2. Has the treatment of the texture of materials, planting, and street furniture been integrated into the overall design?

I. *Urban Esthetics*

1. Does the proposal include works of art such as fountains, sculpture, textures, painting?
2. Does it include integrated and applied decoration and other human amenities?
3. Does the proposal present a visual total satisfying to human emotional needs?

INDEX

This book is one of a series published under the auspices of the Joint Center for Urban Studies, a cooperative venture of the Massachusetts Institute of Technology and Harvard University. The Joint Center was founded in 1959 to organize and encourage research on urban and regional problems. Participants have included scholars from the fields of anthropology, architecture, business, city planning, economics, education, engineering, history, law, philosophy, political science, and sociology.

The findings and conclusions of this book are, as with all Joint Center publications, solely the responsibility of the author.

Other books published in the Joint Center series include:

Harvard University Press

The Intellectual Versus the City: From Jefferson to Frank Lloyd Wright, Morton and Lucia White, 1962.

Streetcar Suburbs, Sam B. Warner, Jr., 1962.

City Politics, Edward C. Banfield and James Q. Wilson, 1963.

Law and Land: Anglo-American Planning Practice, Charles M. Haar, editor, 1964.

Location and Land Use, William Alonso, 1964.

Poverty and Progress, Stephan Thernstrom, 1964.

Boston: The Job Ahead, Martin Meyerson and Edward C. Banfield, 1966.

The Myth and Reality of Our Urban Problems, Raymond Vernon, 1966.

Muslim Cities in the Later Middle Ages, Ira Marvin Lapidus, 1967.

The Fragmented Metropolis: Los Angeles, 1850–1930, Robert M. Fogelson, 1967.

Law and Equal Opportunity: A Study of the Massachusetts Commission Against Discrimination, Leon H. Mayhew, 1968.

Varieties of Police Behavior: The Management of Law and Order in Eight Communities, James Q. Wilson, editor, 1968.

The Metropolitan Enigma: Inquiries into the Nature and Dimensions of America's "Urban Crisis," James Q. Wilson, editor, 1968.

Traffic and the Police: Variations in Law-Enforcement Policy, John A. Gardiner, 1969.

The M.I.T. Press

The Image of the City, Kevin Lynch, 1960.

Housing and Economic Progress: A Study of the Housing Experiences of Boston's Middle-Income Families, Lloyd Rodwin, 1961.

The Historian and the City, Oscar Handlin and John E. Burchard, editors, 1963.

Beyond the Melting Pot: The Negroes, Puerto Ricans, Jews, Italians, and Irish of New York City, Nathan Glazer and Daniel P. Moynihan, 1963.

The Future of Old Neighborhoods: Rebuilding for a Changing Population, Bernard J. Frieden, 1964.

Man's Struggle for Shelter in an Urbanizing World, Charles Abrams, 1964.

The Federal Bulldozer: A Critical Analysis of Urban Renewal, 1949–1962, Martin Anderson, 1964.

The View from the Road, Donald Appleyard, Kevin Lynch, and John R. Myer, 1964.

The Public Library and the City, Ralph W. Conant, editor, 1965.

Urban Renewal: The Record and the Controversy, James Q. Wilson, editor, 1966.

Regional Development Policy: A Case Study of Venezuela, John Friedmann, 1966.

Transport Technology for Developing Regions: A Study of Road Transportation in Venezuela, Richard M. Soberman, 1966.

Computer Methods in the Analysis of Large-Scale Social Systems, James M. Beshers, editor, 1968.

Planning Urban Growth and Regional Development: The Experience of the Guayana Program of Venezuela, Lloyd Rodwin and Associates, 1969.

Build a Mill, Build a City, Build a School: Industrialization, Urbanization, and Education in Ciudad Guayana, Noel F. McGinn and Russell G. Davis, 1969.

Land-Use Controls in the United States, second edition, John Delafons, 1969.

DATE DUE

5|3|01